VENTURESOME LOVE

The Story of Constance Hornby
1884 – 1972

Elizabeth Traill

British Library Cataloguing in Publication Data:
a catalogue record for this publication
is available from the British Library

ISBN   978-1-871828-72-6

Typeset in 11 pt. Palatino Linotype
at 35 Dunbar Rd, Haddington

Print and Cover by Westport Print and Design,
St Andrews

and printed in Uganda by
Makerere University Printery, Kampala

CONTENTS

DEDICATION

To the memory of my dear parents,
David and Maxine Traill

FOREWORD

I am delighted to be writing this foreword on behalf of the many generations of women and whole communities in Uganda who have benefited from Miss Hornby's sacrifical and venturesome love.

Although I was born and brought up in the Eastern region of Uganda, and Miss Hornby served mainly in the Western region, I feel I am part of her story. I have so many connections with Miss Hornby! Her family came from the North of England, where I now live; there people appreciate straight talking and speak their minds. In the early '80s my husband served his curacy years in a church on the edge of Richmond Park, where Miss Hornby grew up and went to school and spent her formative years. Bishop Festo Kivengere took our wedding, and he and his wife Merab always gave us sound advice and brotherly and sisterly love; and I was at Gayaza High School with Charity and Hope, their daughters, again where Miss Hornby taught briefly. Prior to that I went to Iganga Girls' Boarding School for my primary education – again, Miss Hornby's first posting. So I already feel connected and close to the story of Miss Hornby, not least because I knew many of the people mentioned in this book.

A pioneer minister is someone who opens new possibilities to create Christian community with and for people who are currently outside the church. Constance Hornby was such a person in every sense of the word, though I am not sure whether she knew it. A pioneer needs boldness and the ability to create, under God, something new. Miss Hornby was far sighted in seeing the potential of educating the girl child at a time when many in society thought it was a waste of time and money. She was hugely rewarded in that she found the girls to be highly motivated and hardworking, and well worth investing in. There is a divine dissatisfaction with the status quo and a willingness to take risks with a new vision and new developments. A pioneer is a catalyst for change, ready to provoke all areas of the church and community to serious questioning. Pioneers are continually pushing the boundaries from the inside. Pioneers are always going to be opening up new possibilities, and that is not always easy for the institution.

In order to be an effective pioneer, one needs a robust spiritual life; pioneers need to love people and be with people where they are; they must have the capacity to be resilient and be fairly thick-skinned to be able to follow God's call to a new place. Constance Hornby's Abrahamic faith was just that. There was a willingness and a restlessness about her to follow God to wherever he led her. Pioneers are risk-takers and besides praying, they are good at identifying and helping develop other pioneers. Miss Hornby nurtured and encouraged many other young women to take on leadership roles. She was a natural evangelist and pioneer: "a practical Christian missionary, totally devoted to serving her Lord and master and helping his people." Her life's work was truly shaped by God. She was loved and accepted by the people she served and she also allowed herself to be changed by them. Her calling was truly incarnational, relational and proclaimed God's unconditional and venturesome love to all humankind. Miss Hornby was a woman ahead of her time and an excellent role model for many women in our world today.

Margaret Sentamu
Bishopthorpe,
York,
England

ACKNOWLEDGEMENTS

From the beginning, Rev. Peter Rwabyoma gave me a lot of useful advice. He was born and brought up in Kigezi District, trained for the ordained ministry in the Church of Uganda and is now lecturing in Mass Communication at Bishop Barham University College, Kabale. The "Quest for the Historic Hornby", as we termed it, began in 2002, thirty years after her death and drew us ever onwards. Together we conducted interviews of people who remembered her and circulated Questionnaires. The results have been included in the later chapters of this book.

The Bishop of Kigezi, Rt Rev. George Katwesigye, and his team fully support the production of this book. The Diocesan Secretary, Canon George Tumwine, and the Education Secretary, Rev. Robert Kayongwe, are enthusiastic. Mrs Evelyn Kasaaza, Chairperson of the Hornby High School Old Girls' Association has given valuable information. Professor Edward Rugumayo and his wife Foibe, whose mother was one of Miss Hornby's girls, have made a written contribution. Advice has also come from Professor Manuel Muranga, Principal, and other staff and students at Bishop Barham University College, Kabale. Philip Tibenderana, engineer in the Water Department, Diocese of Kigezi, kindly traced the original Kabira Mission Station Plan, which had turned brown with age. Some valuable old photographs taken by Dr Len Sharp, now in the care of B.B.U.C. Library, were scanned by Simon Rwabyoma. The list could go on, but lastly two old friends of Miss Hornby who live in Kinkiizi must be mentioned. Canon William and Schola Mbarubukeye used to host her for visits to that area and have a fund of memories.

The early years of Constance Hornby's life story had to rely upon research in Britain, much of it in the style of a detective story, gathering clues and investigating leads. We had to work back from the 'known', that is, memories and records of her latter years, to the 'unknown' period from childhood in London to her arrival in Uganda in 1916. The Archivist of the Church Mission Society, Ken Osborne, made available a full set of the magazine *Ruanda Notes* and some confidential papers dating from 1914-15 when Constance Hornby was training for missionary service. He gave great help and support over the years of research. The Librarian of the Women's Library in London allowed the author access to the Girls' Friendly Society Magazines during the period when she was their "Own Missionary". Constance Hornby had a lively style of letter-writing and the author has drawn upon numerous letters to prayer partners and supporters, published by the Ruanda Mission, C.M.S., and the G.F.S. The two maps have been reproduced with the kind permission of Dr Grace Carswell, lecturer in Human Geography, University of Sussex, and drawn by their Cartography Department.

To all those who have helped and encouraged me, I wish to express deep gratitude. My dear brother, Ian, and my sister-in-law, Fiona, have stood behind me throughout the years of annual pilgrimage to Uganda. All the younger members of my family have been very good to me. Special thanks should go to Ann Farrow who helped me to find "King's Farm" on a map, to Madge Quinn who shared a house in Kabale with me from 1967 onwards, to Jean Hurford, Dr Chris and Margaret Scruby, Rev. Tim and Barbara Oakley, Jennie Tustian, Dudley and Margaret Carr, Margaret Walker, Elisabeth Abraham and others who knew Miss Hornby in her last years. Rev. Sister Josie Midwinter helped with the research and contacted her Church Army friend Ann Morisy for permission to use the term *Venturesome Love* as the title. It was willingly given. Mrs Margaret Stevens provided two old maps which had belonged to her father, Mr Clement Pain, former headmaster of Mbarara High School. Other people have filled in questionnaire forms and answered questions. Friends in St Baldred's Church, North Berwick helped me through a time of writer's block and advised a holiday. Margaret Heavenor, Margaret Anderson, Jill Farrow, Fiona MacLean and Sheelagh Warren gave valuable advice about the text. Mrs Diana MacNaughton gave me a copy of *Journeying Out* by Ann Morisy. Mr Roger F.L. Wilkins, former headmaster of Kigezi College, Butobere, and later Country Director of British Council, Kampala, made available some fascinating photographs. Lastly, Revs Jock and Margaret Stein have given great encouragement and practical expertise in preparing the book for publication.

The writing has been a long task but well worthwhile. We all loved Constance Hornby and we wish to make her story more widely known. All glory to Jesus our great Master, *"Rabboni"*, who inspired her to go to Uganda as a young woman and worked through her to the benefit of thousands of women, girls and other people.

Liz Traill
North Berwick,
February 2011

INTRODUCTION

"Kigezi Girls' No. 1 Teacher"[1]

Constance Hornby was the pioneer of education for women and girls in Kigezi, in the mountainous South-West of Uganda. Her legacy remains in many Christian homes and in the lives of her Old Girls, their children and grandchildren. Hornby High School, Kabale, was named after her. Her pioneering work was also part of a wider movement to uplift the position of women world-wide. She was an advocate of justice for the poor and under-privileged. Ann Morisy says in her book that "Venturesome Love" is the motivation for embracing a struggle for the benefit of others.[2] It is chosen as the title because Constance Hornby certainly embraced a hard life so that the women and girls of Kigezi would know something better. Another book relevant to her overall strategy is *Lifestyle Evangelism* by Joe Aldrich who explains Biblical principles of effective mission through living amongst the people.

There are very few written records of her early life. It would have been easier for the author and her friends if she had left diaries or journals upon which the story could be based. Instead, we have collected information through interviews, articles, Census records and books written by others. She made an impact as a remarkable character, leaving many stories to be told, and delight to be found in her unique sense of humour. She is still talked about in the churches, schools and homes of Kigezi today. There is a great demand for this book in Uganda where Church leaders have requested a record of her life to pass on to the younger generation.

Personal experience of meeting her

This is what we knew. Miss Hornby retired from her active missionary service in Uganda at the end of October 1954 and in 1956 she went to live in a warm, fertile corner of her beloved Kigezi District. She lived

---

[1] Title of newspaper article in the *Uganda Argus*, August 25th 1969.
[2] Morisy, Ann, page 32.

contentedly in retirement for ten years in Kinkiizi County. In 1966, the newly elected first Bishop of Kigezi, Rev. Dick Lyth, decided that she should be brought to live in Kabale, the Diocesan centre, so that she could be cared for in her old age more adequately. She made new friends amongst our group of young expatriate teachers at Kigezi High School and Kabale Preparatory School. We used to visit her after school. She said, *"When I came to Kigezi, there was not a girl who knew 'A' from a Bumble Bee. Now, I have five grandchildren at Makerere University!"* Her quick-witted conversation was delightful. *"I have tea with bread and butter, not cake"*, she used to say. Home-made pots of jam were appropriate gifts for her 81st and 82nd birthdays in 1967 and 1968. She cheerfully admitted that during her ten years in Kinkiizi no one thought about birthdays and she could not remember the year when she was born! She knew the date, October 4th, and stated that the year was 1886. One day the District Medical Officer, Dr Dick Vinden, as the local Representative for the British High Commission, had reason to check Miss Hornby's passport and saw that the year of her birth was actually 1884. Everyone was astonished and amused to hear that she was in fact two years older than she thought! Her next birthday, October 4th 1969, was her 85th! The confusion lingered in the minds of friends and amongst the wider public long after her death in 1972. To establish the truth became one part of the research.

Research in Surrey

It was necessary to go to the Surrey History Centre in Woking and to the Local History Centre in Richmond to study some original documents. I am grateful to Elizabeth Abbott for making the arrangements for me. The town of Richmond is on the Southern side of the River Thames about ten miles South-West of the centre of London. First, a search was made in the England National Census of 1901, but the necessary details were not found although it confirmed that Constance Hornby was living somewhere in Surrey in that year. The Census of 1891 was not initially productive. We had been told that she was born at King's Farm, Richmond, Surrey, but the farm itself no longer exists in the twenty-first century. A Street Atlas of London dating from the 1930's provided a clue, namely *King's Farm Road, Richmond.* Finally, the current *A-Z Guide to London* showed a Church of England Primary School built on the open space which was once the Farm, named after the Parish Church of Holy Trinity. A careful search in the original Baptismal Register of Holy Trinity Church at last yielded the desired

When Baptized.	Child's Christian Name.	Parents' Names. Christian.	Surname.	Abode.	Quality, Trade, or Profession.	By whom the Ceremony was performed.
1884 Oct. 30th Born Sept. 22nd? No. 329	Florence Kate	Alfred Otis	Farrow	5 Prince's Rd	Labourer	Evan H. Hopkins. (Vicar)
1884 Nov. 2nd Born Oct. 4th No. 330	Constance Edith Julia	Henry	Hornby	King's Farm Dairy Farm	[Privately Baptized.]	Edw: Wilcox
1884 Nov. 2nd Born Aug. 6th No. 331	Alice	Frederick William Dawson & Louisa	Farrell	13, Victoria Villas.	Police Constable.	E. Wilcox.

EXTRACT FROM THE BAPTISM REGISTER OF HOLY TRINITY CHURCH, RICHMOND.
[REPRODUCED BY PERMISSION OF SURREY HISTORY CENTRE]

information. Baby Constance, one month old, was baptized on 2nd November 1884 by Rev. Edward Wilcox. Her parents' names were Mr Henry Epton Hornby and his wife Julia. His occupation was "Dairyman" and the address was "King's Farm". It was an exciting discovery. More insights followed. The same Register recorded Constance's older sister, Lucy Mary, born March 13th 1883 and her younger brother named Henry Epton after their father, born January 4th 1890.

The 1891 Census was searched again, this time by an expert at the Richmond Local History Centre. The Hornby family was found at King's Farm with the names of the parents and five children, also a governess and a general servant. The local environment at the time was further illustrated by the 1894 Ordnance Survey Map and a number of photographs taken in the area. A delightful pencil drawing entitled "King's Farm" was also found. The farmhouse had a tiled roof. A visit to Holy Trinity Church provided the opportunity to fill in the background to Constance's spiritual development.

PENCIL SKETCH OF KING'S FARM – MAYBE THE HOUSE WHERE
CONSTANCE HORNBY WAS BORN.
[USED BY PERMISSION OF RICHMOND LOCAL STUDIES COLLECTION]

Guiding Question

This was our guiding question about her early years: what were the factors which shaped her character and prepared her for the tough life of a pioneer missionary in the heart of Africa? We invite you to board a time capsule and travel back more than 120 years to England in Victorian times. The motor car was yet to appear on the streets; telephone, aeroplane and wireless were in the process of invention. Constance Hornby lived her whole life without a mobile phone or computer but she knew all about prayer and direct communication with her Lord and Master. She did not have access to the Internet or to a big library, but she did know her Bible very well and she had that special inner wisdom which derives from the fear and love of the Lord. We send out this account of a life well-lived in faith and obedience to him, with prayer that the same Lord will use it for his glory and the extension of his kingdom in the future.

CONSTANCE HORNBY, 1931
["RUANDA NOTES", C.M.S. ARCHIVES]

Chapter One
1884 – 1901
EARLY LIFE

Setting the scene

Richmond, Surrey, on the western outskirts of London, was a fashionable place in the Victorian era. It had strong royal connections going back to King Edward I (1272-1307). A royal palace was built here by King Henry VII in 1500 and his granddaughter Elizabeth I died here in 1603. The palace was in ruins by the time of Queen Victoria (1837-1901) but the nearby hunting park, like a small game park with deer and other animals roaming wild, was an attraction. At the northern end of the park was a large farm (225 acres) established by King Charles I (1625-49). The King's Farm was a special interest of King George III (1760-1820), who kept sheep, cows, oxen and horses. By the 1880s, it had developed into primarily a dairy farm. During the industrial revolution the railway to Reading and the west of England reached Richmond in 1846. Housing development took place rapidly as London extended outwards. Amongst other gems of historical information is the comment, *"the pine-apple was first cultivated at Richmond"*. The great Botanic Gardens at Kew lie on the same side of the River Thames, within walking distance of King's Farm.

The Hornby family at home

Constance was born on 4ᵗʰ October, 1884, second child of Mr Henry Epton Hornby and his wife Julia, at their home on King's Farm. This formed the northern section of Richmond Park, across the Sheen Road. Her older sister, Lucy Mary, was a toddler, born in March the previous year at a different address in Richmond. Their father was a dairyman, looking after the milking cows on the large Farm. The children would have seen parts of the eight mile wall surrounding the Park and many tall chestnut trees, with leaves like huge hands. They bore shiny brown conkers in the autumn, providing for endless childhood games. They would also see steam trains passing along the railway nearby. The family grew as William (1886), Wilifred (1888) and Henry Epton Junior (1890) were born. We believe that another daughter was born after the 1891 Census, but this has not been confirmed yet.

Victorians normally had large families. The Hornbys with six children, four girls and two boys, would be unexceptional. Like Uganda in the twenty-first century, the population of England in the nineteenth century was growing rapidly with a steady drift to the towns and cities. People were on the move from the countryside into the urban areas because agriculture was becoming mechanized and foreign trade, especially the cheaper wheat from America, was upsetting the local markets. The building of railways in a network all over the country facilitated transport. The Hornby family came from the North of England. Records show that Henry Epton Hornby and his wife Julia were both born in Lincolnshire, a wheat-growing area. They were probably farmers and, on moving to Richmond, may have been associated with Hornby's Stables on Lonsdale Terrace, where Lucy Mary was born in 1883. Perhaps the Stables were run by Mr Hornby's brother. Stables were a familiar feature of towns in those days. A number of horses would be stalled by night and would work by day pulling the cabs, coaches, carriages and horse buses which were the equivalent of taxis and minibuses today.

Constance's father helped to supply the demand for fresh milk to the growing population of London. While the cows were grazing on the green fields of King's Farm, Mr Hornby may have taken the morning and evening milk in churns around the town in a horse-drawn dray, stopping outside people's homes. Servants from the big houses in Richmond would come out to collect the milk in jugs. Centralised dairies and refrigeration came after this time.

By April 1891 when the National Census was taken, the Hornby Family was established in Audley House on King's Farm. Mr Hornby was now a "Dairyman/Farmer". Lucy Mary, Constance and William[1] were "Scholars". Wilifred and Henry Epton Jr were too young to start schooling. The family had a general servant named Ellen Carpenter, a single lady, and a governess named Eliza K. Norris, also a single lady.

---

[1] Each of these three children was born at a different address in Richmond. In 1883 the family lived at No. 6 Lonsdale Terrace. Next to that address, according to the 1901 Census, were *Hornby's Stables*. It would seem that Constance came from a family of animal handlers. They did not own the Farm where she was born; her father looked after the cows and milked them.

The household thus consisted of nine people. Mr and Mrs Hornby must have preferred home schooling rather than sending the three older children to local schools. Miss Hornby herself told us that she did not go to school until she was nine years old (1893) and that she used to sell eggs at the end of King's Farm Road. The very spot may be seen today, sheltered by tall chestnut trees which would have been saplings when she was a girl. She received some education before the age of nine. Indeed she would have learned her "three Rs" (reading, writing

END OF KING'S FARM RD, WITH CHESTNUT TREES *[E. TRAILL 2006]*

and arithmetic) very well under Miss Norris' tutelage at home. The family was thus moderately well-off; they were respectable people. Their life-style may be illustrated by considering two contemporary

On the
Sheen
Rd in
1890

[Pictures reproduced by permission of the London Borough of Richmond upon Thames Local Studies Library]

Coach
and
four
horses
on the
Sheen
Rd in
1890

photographs of Sheen Road in 1890. They show large brick-built houses with several chimneys, indicating that there were coal fires in every room. Gas street lighting illuminated the road at night. Each house had a front garden with a wall or fence and a gate. As for means of transport, there is no sign of any motorcar, although that invention was soon to transform the whole system. Instead, there is a man on horseback and a fine coach and four horses with a number of people on board. A lady with a long dress and a wide hat is standing at the side of the road with an early perambulator. All the people in the photographs are smartly dressed, including hats.

The country life and parish church

Thus far, two factors influencing Constance's upbringing may be traced. First, she came from a solid, hard-working family. Her father's work would have brought her into early contact with animals and farming practices. Although she lived on the outskirts of London, she had the healthy upbringing of a country girl and was not afraid of hard physical work for long hours. Secondly, her family moved house at least twice in her early childhood. Her parents had moved from faraway Lincolnshire to London in their youth. Therefore perhaps she had wanderlust within her from the start. She would not fear packing up and moving across the world. Life in other places probably interested her. She had no deep roots in a particular place in England. Indeed, later on Uganda became her home and the hardworking Bakiga farmers "her" people.

Another major influence in her life came through the local Church. King's Farm[2] lay within the Parish of a newly established "mission" Church built to serve the outlying new houses and estates to the east of Richmond Town. Both rich and poor lived in the parish. The Richmond Union Workhouse where destitute people were fed, housed and given work under supervision was only about a mile from the Hornbys' home. In that section of the Parish congested streets with tightly packed small houses were under construction. Along the main road there were large houses with gardens. Holy Trinity Church was built to accommodate

---

[2] By 1911 when an Ordnance Survey Map was published, King's Farm had been sold and broken up into small gardens or allotments. Many more houses were built. A railway crosses the northern end of what was King's Farm, with North Sheen Station on the boundary.

800 people, a beautiful building with a tower. It was consecrated in June 1870 and Rev. Evan Henry Hopkins was inducted as the first Vicar. He was the son of a mining engineer, converted to Christ when he was a student of Engineering. He preached with exceptional clarity and spiritual power, drawing hundreds of people to the Sunday services. Outreach meetings during the week touched many more. The new

EVAN HENRY HOPKINS (1837-1918)
[BY PERMISSION OF HOLY TRINITY CHURCH, RICHMOND]

Church pulsated with spiritual life. The Vicar was involved in the founding of the Church Army, also the Keswick Convention.

The Hornby family was probably amongst the regular congregation. They certainly had their children baptized at Holy Trinity Church. Services would have followed the Book of Common Prayer (1662) and so when Constance was baptized by Rev. Edward Wilcox on November 2nd 1884 at the age of one month, these prophetic words were prayed for her: that she might be *"steadfast in faith, joyful through hope and rooted in charity"*. Infant baptism was just the beginning of her Christian upbringing. At home, in common with most Victorian Christians, Mr Hornby would have conducted Family Prayers every evening. She would have heard Bible stories, learned about Jesus and said her prayers from an early age. When old enough to go to Sunday School, she would have joined one of the many classes at Holy Trinity Church.

The beginnings of the Church Army

The Vicar was full of evangelistic zeal and concern for all the people in his parish. He saw that there were many who were outside the reach of the established church because of their poverty or their antisocial behaviour. He longed for them to know the love of God in Jesus Christ. When he heard about the work of General William Booth in Whitechapel, part of London's East End, and the founding of The Salvation Army, he was inspired. He visited Whitechapel several times, about twelve miles from Richmond, and studied the structure of The Salvation Army. Then, with his wife's support, he set up the "Church Gospel Army" in Holy Trinity Church in 1881 on similar lines.

One young leader of the outreach work was Wilson Carlile, a businessman whose family belonged to the Church. He was greatly influenced by Rev. Evan Henry Hopkins' teaching and example and in 1878 he decided to leave the family business of trading in silk to seek ordination into the ministry. He served his curacy in St Mary Abbots Church in Kensington and there in 1882, he founded the Church Army by drawing together three projects, namely the "Gospel Army" in Richmond, secondly an off-shoot "Gospel Army" in Oxford run by a student who was a member of Holy Trinity, and thirdly the "Church Mission Army" at a church in Bristol. The movement grew despite opposition and served working class people and those on the margins of society. The leaders were drawn from the ranks and given training.

The Church Army became the largest lay society in the Church of England, recognized for its evangelistic and social work. It is now established in many parts of the world, the U.S.A., Australia, New Zealand, East Africa and other Commonwealth countries. For his services, Rev. Wilson Carlile was appointed Prebendary of St Paul's Cathedral, London, in 1906. He died at the great age of 95 in 1942.[3]

Constance as a young girl in the late 1880's would have seen the members of the Church Army at the 11 o'clock service, fresh from an open air meeting. The men and boys were a very enthusiastic group who enjoyed singing hymns and were prone to slap their thighs and exclaim "Hallelujah!" loudly at key points in the Vicar's sermons. This upset some more staid members of the regular congregation and so the Vicar had to caution the enthusiasts. After the service, a Men's Bible Class followed and then the Army marched behind a banner with a band playing cheerful hymn tunes along the Sheen Road and northwards to the Mission Hall on Lower Mortlake Road, probably up Manor Road along the edge of King's Farm. We can imagine little Constance with the other Hornby children and their parents on a Sunday afternoon walk watching the band go by. Constance was very observant and retained the image of Christian people being soldiers in Christ's army all her life. She taught generations of girls in Uganda to sing one of her favourite hymns based on this metaphor.[4]

God's early call to the mission field

There was always an emphasis on young people's work within the ministry of Rev. Evan Henry Hopkins. He was an evangelist who called those responding to the Gospel to full consecration, faith in Christ and obedience in daily life. We do not know exactly when Constance received Jesus into her heart, but we are told that she heard God's call to be a missionary at the age of 11, in the year 1895. It may be significant that Rev. Evan Henry Hopkins moved to a Church in Kensington in 1893 and a new Vicar of Holy Trinity was received. Rev. H.C. Squires

---

[3] Information about Rev. Wilson Carlile gleaned from the Oxford Dictionary of National Biography, 2004.

[4] Hymn 230 in the Runyankore-Rukiga Prayer Book, is based on "We are soldiers of Christ, who is mighty to save" by Thomas Pollock, Supplemental Hymns to Hymns Ancient and Modern, 1889. See Appendix Two.

had served as a missionary in Bombay, India. Perhaps he stressed the needs of the wider world in his sermons, or there may have been special "Missionary Meetings" at the Church attended by the young people.

The call to full surrender preached by Rev. Evan Henry Hopkins had led a number of key workers at Holy Trinity Church to offer for missionary service. They went to Smyrna, Algiers, China, Pondoland in Transkei, South Africa, Kikuyu in Kenya, Nigeria and Persia. Doubtless, the prayers and gifts of members of the Church supported them. Constance would have been aware of the doings of these missionaries as she grew up. One of them, Miss E. May Grimes was a well-known hymn writer whose songs were used at the Keswick Convention. The best known is *"Speak Lord in the stillness, while I wait on Thee"*. She also wrote,

> The Master comes! He calls for thee –
> go forth at His almighty word;
> obedient to His last command;
> and tell to those who never heard,
> who sit in deepest shades of night,
> that Christ has come to give them light!
>
> The Master calls! Shall not thy heart
> in warm responsive love reply,
> "Lord, here am I, send me, send me –
> thy willing slave – to live or die;
> an instrument unfit indeed,
> yet Thou wilt give me what I need."
>
> *(Keswick Hymn Book, no. 408)*

Miss Grimes herself received a missionary calling and she went to Pondoland, in Transkei.[5] Young Constance at the age of eleven sometime in 1895 heard and answered God's personal call to go to another land in the service of Christ. She could well have sung this hymn herself as that was how she spoke of her wholehearted relationship with Christ in her old age. Wise people in her Church took care of her spiritual development.

---

[5] Pondoland was mentioned by Nelson Mandela as the birthplace of anti-apartheid leading lawyer Oliver Tambo who was the product of a Mission school. See *Long Walk to Freedom* p. 55. Teachers usually have little knowledge of what their pupils will achieve in future.

The Keswick Convention, its speakers and teaching would have been well known to them all. The Vicar of Holy Trinity, Richmond, Rev. Evan Henry Hopkins was one of the original team when it opened in 1875 and he attended for forty years. It is possible that Constance went with a party from her Church to attend the annual Convention Week whenever she could as she grew up. God was preparing her in every way for her life's work and ministry.

St John's Infants' School, Richmond, Daily Timetable

9.00 - 9.10   Assembly and Prayers
9.10 - 9.20   Registers marked
9.20 - 9.50   Religious Instruction
9.50 - 10.00   Registers finally closed
10.00-10.10   Physical Exercise
The day continued in 30-minute lessons: Number, Reading, Writing, Observation/Nature, Singing, before the Lunch Hour. The afternoon began with Registration followed by Varied Occupations, Drawing, Singing and Games.
4.05 – 4.10   Dismissal

Victorian primary schools

Educational methods were developing during Constance's childhood. In 1880 an Act of Parliament made Elementary Education compulsory in England and Wales and in 1891 school fees were abolished in most primary-level schools. Places in secondary schools were limited.[6] The expensive fee-paying "public" schools were for the upper classes in Victorian society, the "grammar" schools charged lower fees and were more accessible to middle and working-class people. The fact that Constance attended a boarding school and a secondary school for girls puts her into the minority of girls who received the basic secondary education in her day. She must have come from a family which saw the advantages of educating girls and had the means to support her through school.

We do not know much about Constance's school education from the age of nine. Initially to gain some information about Primary or

---

[6]   The Encyclopedia Britannica (2007) Vol 18, p. 57 says, "In 1900 one child in 70 could expect to enter a secondary school of some kind."

Elementary Schools in Richmond at the time, three original School Log Books were consulted at the Surrey History Centre. No Class Registers or Enrolment records were available to check whether she attended one of these schools. Only a general impression was obtained. The St John's Infants' School Log, a large leather-bound book with a brass clasp and lock and clear handwriting on every page, includes the Daily Timetable on the page opposite.

Attendance at that School must have been generally problematic and irregular.

Another Log Book, that of the British Infant School, noted frequent poor attendance due to Whooping Cough, Influenza, heavy Colds and FOG (written in capital letters). A fog could last for several days enveloping London and its outskirts in a thick, smoky damp blanket of air. It formed mainly on calm days in winter and was thickened by the smoke from thousands of household and factory chimneys, all burning coal. Visibility was minimal. It was very unpleasant and unhealthy. Transport was brought to a standstill. It caused chest complaints, coughs and breathing difficulties. Londoners suffered from occasional fogs throughout the Victorian era and until some years after the Second World War, when the Clean Air Acts were implemented. Miss Hornby mentioned FOG in one of her letters, recalling her childhood experience:

On Trek in Bufumbira: November 1st 1931 (All Saints' Day)

What do you think I should like better than anything else just now? There are three things. Can you guess? They are first of all a fog – a thick still fog. Why? Well, here the wind never stops blowing, and the dust hurts your eyes more than fog. As I sit and write to you now in this wee hut, I keep blowing the dust off my paper. Now, if there were a fog, there would be no dust, and the trees would be still and the house would be quiet.

Secondly, I should like some hairpins. I've only five left, and there is no hope of getting more for nine days. I forgot to ask for them when my man took the letters yesterday.

Thirdly, I should like a big roasted apple, an apple with the white inside bursting out of the brown skin. Since I started this trek on October 1st I've only been able to get potatoes, dried peas and beans to eat. No fruit, only the sort that comes out of tins.

The Log Book of Richmond British Girls' School 1870-1907 had a list of subjects taught: Poetry, Animal Physiology, Drawing, Needlework, Domestic Economy and Singing by Rote. They had Object Lessons on the timetable, when a teacher would hold up a sample and tell its story to the children: Nuts, Salt, Tea, Coal and Money. Maps were studied of the Political and Physical Geography of Europe and doubtless the vast spread of the British Empire, coloured pink on Mercator's projection. Emphasis was placed on memory work and drill. There was little scope for original thinking by the children. Child-centred education had not yet penetrated to the majority of schools.

Education was a serious business. School discipline was very strict. The Headmistress of Richmond Girls' School wrote one day, *"Children docile and intelligent."* This summarized what she and her colleagues had achieved. Victorian children were expected to be quiet, well-mannered and neatly dressed. Idleness was frowned upon. The girls became expert in needlework, embroidery, crochet, lace-making, bead-work and other skills. They learned how to make their own clothes, with or without the use of a newly-invented sewing machine. Constance had the experience of her own schooling to draw upon when she began to teach girls in Uganda. It is not surprising that her girls were well-disciplined and were taught the same skills that she had imbibed in her childhood. Beadwork, crochet and embroidery are still carried on by young girls in Uganda, whereas twenty-first century British girls are more likely to know how to use computers and mobile phones than needle and thread.

Education was fundamental to Victorian society. The conquest of illiteracy in the whole country was a primary objective. The system of Pupil Teachers was developed, whereby selected older children were given extra lessons and then expected to teach what they had learnt to younger children. After five years they could go on to Teacher Training College and gain a full qualification.[7] If it is true that Constance did not attend school until she was nine years old (1893), it must have been for

---

[7] According to the *Encyclopaedia Britannica (2007) Vol. 18,* the system of Pupil Teachers replaced the earlier Monitorial System in England around 1840 as a method of economy (it reduced the number of adult teachers needed) and efficiency (it avoided wasting the time of children who waited for the attention of the principal teacher). After 5 years' apprenticeship from the age of 13, during which time they learned the art of teaching and were paid a small weekly sum, the Pupil Teachers could enter a normal school or training college which combined professional and academic training.

reasons other than inability to pay the fees. Presumably "home schooling" under the Hornby governess Miss Eliza K. Norris was accepted by the School Inspectors. When she did enter school, her experience would tally with the basic Education described since the same standards and practices were maintained in all the schools.

The patchwork of teaching: one pupil's revealing experience

Teacher Training was at its early stage of development. Many teachers working in the schools had no formal training at all. Sometimes the Elementary school teachers themselves did not understand the principles behind what they were teaching. For illustration, we can refer to the fascinating autobiography of another contemporary London schoolgirl named Molly Hughes.[8] Molly became a trained teacher and so her comments and reflections on Education are valid. Her family lived in North London. Her father worked long hours in an office, but her mother stayed at home with the children and proved highly inspirational, opening their minds to the treasures of education in the broad sense. She even took them on expeditions to explore the riverbank at Richmond, collecting conkers from the chestnut trees and watching the cheerful boats on the Thames! Molly was sent to a typical Elementary School and wrote some rather disparaging comments: *"Division: no one bothered about method or understanding as long as you got the answer. I have no recollection of any timetable at School. In Religious Instruction it was usual to do a little Scripture every morning. This consisted of writing out and reciting a verse or two, fortunately without any religious comment."* Molly was happy to win a place at secondary level at the new North London Collegiate School for Girls under the great pioneering Headmistress, Miss Buss. It was run on similar lines to a boys' Public School, providing a classical education. Having survived several years of intense study and strong discipline enforced by the Prefect system, she entered the relative freedom of the Sixth Form. Molly noticed that the teachers tended to be totally absorbed by the life of the School and not encouraged to have outside interests. She went on to Cambridge to train as a teacher, with the warm support of Miss Buss herself. Her book is an entertaining account of another London girl's experience at the time when Constance was growing up.

---

[8]   See Bibliography for details of *A London Family 1870-1900*.

The British Empire was expanding

It is likely that Constance in her teenage years took an interest in the wider world and would have heard something about the remote area in the heart of Africa known as Uganda. In 1894, when she was ten, a British Protectorate was declared following years of philanthropic and commercial work by the Imperial British East Africa Company. One of Company's avowed aims was to stop the continuing slave trade in East Africa. The growth of trade and development depended on improved communication and transport. A plan to build the Uganda Railway (dubbed "The Lunatic Express" by some) was hotly debated in the Houses of Parliament and even Britain's involvement in Uganda was disputed. Sir Gerald Portal, Consul General in Zanzibar, was sent to Uganda in 1892 to assess the situation on the ground.

A clever cartoon appeared in the London magazine *Punch* on October 27th 1892, depicting Uganda as "an unmanageable but indispensable white elephant",[10] insinuating that the Company could not handle Uganda. Another *Punch* cartoon (April 21st 1894) depicted a defenceless African baby in a basket left on the steps of the Foreign Office, about to be adopted by the British Government.[9] The Uganda Protectorate was rather reluctantly declared in June 1894 when the Company's work was taken over by the Government. In 1895-96 the decision was finally made to build a railway from Mombasa to Lake Victoria. Work began despite many practical difficulties. These developments would have been followed by the members of Holy Trinity Church, Richmond, and other like-minded Christians, as pointers for increased missionary endeavour in the expanding Empire.

---

[9] For an opinion on these cartoons, which were typical of the time, see the article by the former deputy Makerere University Librarian, Olivia Mutibwa, entitled "First Cartoons on Uganda in UK Media", published in *New Vision*, the newspaper for CHOGM – the Commonwealth Heads of Government Meeting on November 23rd 2007.

Punch political cartoons like these both influenced British Government policy, and commented on it. Note how the first cartoon, portraying Uganda as a huge and troublesome beast, was followed by another portraying Uganda as a baby needing help.

[10] The quotation is from a book by Charles Miller, *The Lunatic Express* (Macdonald, London 1971).

Chapter Two
1901 – 1916
PREPARATION FOR HER LIFE WORK

The passing of the Victorian era

Throughout her life, Constance was a patriotic person, born and brought up in Queen Victoria's reign. The old Queen died in 1901 and Constance as a young woman of seventeen living in London, would have witnessed her funeral and days of mourning, followed by the accession and Coronation of her eldest son, King Edward V11. He was a flamboyant character breaking social conventions. Victorian strictures were unravelling and a new era opened. Economically, Britain was booming and held a dominating position in world trade. The British Empire was at its zenith.

Travel in the age of steam power became easier by land and sea. The early motor car, still modelled on a carriage, made its appearance and rapidly grew in popularity, despite a law passed in 1902 restricting its speed to only 20 mph (32 kph). Public transport in London was still mostly horse-drawn but motorbuses were beginning to run on main routes. Bicycles were popular for men and women and Constance followed this trend by sometimes using a bicycle in Uganda. Electricity was also invented in these years bringing great changes in the towns, but in the countryside villages and farms continued in their traditional ways with horse-drawn machinery and manual labour common in the fields.

The changing position of women

Constance would have worn a long dress and wide hat for best occasions and modest, tailored clothes for everyday wear. She would have been part of a three-tiered society, upper, middle and lower classes. There was a huge gap between the very rich and the poor. Children without shoes even in winter were common on the streets of London. She was moved by poverty and wanted to make a difference. Also, one outcome of the Edwardian era, the growing empowerment of women, would have affected Constance. Girls' education was steadily improving and this led to young women becoming more independent than their forebears. A strong movement led by Mrs Emmelina Pankhurst campaigned for women to have the right to vote for the first time. The "Suffragettes", as they were called even chained themselves to railings in the heart of London in 1908 and were imprisoned for their actions. The political campaign bore fruit in 1918 when votes for women passed through Parliament and into Law. We do not know how much this political movement influenced Constance, but she would have been aware of it. In fact she became passionate about education for women and girls in Kigezi District, south-west Uganda. She certainly knew how to express her opinions with vigour.[1]

Constance at school

We know from Constance's confidential Application papers held by the Church Mission Society that she was sent to a boarding school from age nine to eleven and then attended Beechcroft College in Richmond, described as a "good private school". Some time in those years the Hornby family moved from King's Farm, Richmond to a house in Twickenham on the other side of the River Thames. They lived at 7 Amyand Park Gardens near the Amyand Hospital which was founded by voluntary contributions in 1879. They were a devout Christian family, putting God first in all things. They attended St

7 AMYAND PARK GARDENS: THE HORNBY FAMILY HOME FROM THE 1890S ONWARDS. *[PHOTO ALFRED PENNINGTON 2010]*

---

[1]   An example is in Dr Joe Church's book *Quest for the Highest* (pages 30 & 44) where she questions his interest in big game hunting.

St John's Hospital, Amyand House.
[Photo E. Traill 2009]

Mary's Church and Constance was confirmed in 1902. Her earlier call at the age of eleven to be a missionary became deeper. She wrote in her Application to C.M.S. in 1914, *"Ever since I was confirmed it has been my great hope to do some work for God in the Mission Field and I have prayed that He would accept my services and give me some work."* Some time after her Confirmation she joined St Stephen's Church, Twickenham and became a zealous worker. Rev. H.M. Sanders, her Vicar, wrote of her in 1914, *"She knows more of her Bible in a simple old-fashioned way than do many."* How did this come about?

At Beechcroft College there was a Branch of the Scripture Union. A teacher named Miss Ethel Keay was the patron of the S.U. Group, which Constance joined. After leaving school, from 1902 onwards, Constance was one of the first members of the S.U. Meeting which Miss Keay held in her drawing room (sitting room) *"for schoolgirls and young ladies"*. Constance was a faithful member for 12 years. She valued her Bible more and more, reading it night and morning. This became her lifelong habit.

Miss Keay promoted missionary interest by encouraging the girls to dress dolls. These dolls, dressed in the costumes of countries where missionaries were active, would have become the treasured possessions of other, younger girls. Constance apparently persuaded her family and friends to help. The money from the sale of dolls would go towards Mission work. Constance heard about the Church Missionary Society during her schooldays and she read the magazine *The Gleaner*. She also read books about pioneer missionaries in Victorian times, including the biography of David Livingstone. Throughout her long life she enjoyed a well-written book. She left a full bookcase in her final home on Rugarama Hill, Kabale. Dudley Carr, one of the young teachers mentioned in the Introduction, is still proud to possess the big book she gave to him, *Birds of the World*.

Her early working life

After leaving school, Constance continued to live at home with the rest of the family. Her father ran a dairy business which supplied milk to households in the Twickenham/Richmond area. Constance worked in the office and did all her father's private accounts and book keeping. This probably involved keeping records of all the milk delivered and the preparation of weekly or monthly bills for the customers. It was time-consuming work, all records carefully written by hand. There were no calculators or computers in those days, but there may have been an early, heavy typewriter and a telephone in the office.

Constance also helped her mother in the house. Her younger sister, Wilifred apparently developed consumption (now known as tuberculosis). There was no cure at that time. A person suffering from TB[2] would have a persistent cough and become very weak. Constance helped her mother to nurse Wilifred at home until she died. When her mother's health broke down, she required extra help from Constance for two years. She improved and Constance could have thought about leaving home and offering for missionary service had not one of her two brothers asked her to go to Hailsham in Sussex where he was setting up a farm.

Constance willingly went to join her brother at Gildridge Farm where she assisted him by keeping house. It was a lonely, strange place with a "haunted" farmhouse. No servant would consent to live in it. Constance, strong in the Lord, said she had no fear. We can imagine her doing the housework cheerfully and taking pleasure in the development of a garden with flowers and vegetables. She learnt to make butter, implying that her brother owned milking cows. She spoke of those years to a reporter of the *Uganda Argus* (August 25th 1969). In addition to making butter, she reared chickens and collected eggs which she used to take to market and on the way back she would buy food for

---

2   Tuberculosis is a bacterial infection which mostly attacks the lungs.

the farmhouse. *"Indeed it was a lonely, hard life for me, but those days were very, very happy."* She was alone in the evenings until her brother came home. He became engaged and at last Constance was set free by his marriage in 1913. She wrote an initial letter to the Church Missionary Society on 12th December 1913 from Gildridge Farm, Hailsham, Sussex. Before going on with her story, another influence in those formative years should be considered.

The Keswick Convention

The development of the Keswick Convention during the Edwardian era also formed part of the background to Constance's life story. Rev. Evan Henry Hopkins, the former Vicar of Holy Trinity, Richmond, became the Chairman in 1900. The annual summer Convention was growing significantly, now using two tents each holding 3,000 people for the week of meetings. To some, the Bible teaching seemed traditional and out of tune with the changes in society, politics, moral standards and general economic progress. Rev. Evan Henry Hopkins started a Prayer Conference for speakers and, later, for other supporters. He also drew up guidelines for speakers to ensure that the full doctrinal themes of the Bible were taught. God was moving in a wonderful way and used a special "Keswick" Convention held in Wales in 1903 to bless six young ministers who became leaders of the Welsh Revival which spread like fire. *"The outstanding feature of those days was the universal, inescapable sense of the presence of God, felt in the Revival gatherings, felt also in the homes, on the streets, in the mines and factories, in the schools, even in the theatres and drinking saloons."* (R.B. Jones quoted by Pollock, *The Keswick Story*, p.164). In the summer of 1905, 300 fiery Welshmen attended the Keswick Convention. Hopes were high that the fire of Revival would then spread through England. The leaders of the Convention struggled to contain the hysterical enthusiasm, to keep order and promote lasting spiritual experience. The 1906 Convention was similar but by 1907 the normal quiet, controlled atmosphere of "Keswick" had been resumed.

How Constance later faced the challenge of Revival in Kigezi

Because Rev. Evan Henry Hopkins was a strong influence in Constance's life from early childhood, did the way that he handled the excesses of the Welsh Revival shape her response to Revival in Kigezi in the 1930s? She wrote then of the Holy Spirit bringing peace and order. She struggled to maintain school discipline: *"A wave of revival came across our part of the world and the school did not miss it. These revivals are all right, but when you get an ignorant people who, in their natural life, can and do work themselves into a frantic state, I feel that we are not doing right just to leave them unguided in such matters as singing hymns far into the night, and attending prayer meetings at all sorts of times . . . I have made a very strict rule that there is to be no singing at night . . ."* (4th July 1939) Neither Constance nor her mentor was against the Revival, as such. Both were spiritually sensitive and in tune with the ways of God, but they could not agree with human-generated sensationalism replacing the quiet work of the Holy Spirit. It is quite possible that she attended the Keswick Convention some years and absorbed its approach, or she would have heard its message at her Church.

The international missionary conferences

The fire of the missionary movement in the churches burned brightly in the years when Constance was growing up. Its influence in the Universities was strong and many young men and women gave up promising careers at home to go and proclaim the Gospel in what was called the non-Christian world. Three big Missionary Conferences were held, in 1888, 1900 and 1910 with the aim of uniting the churches in mission. The Conference at Edinburgh in 1910 was the most influential largely because many leaders coming from different denominations were present and the programme was based upon solid research and study. Eight volumes of reports were produced. However, only 17 out of the 1200 delegates at the Conference came from the new churches in the "mission fields". Outdated ideas and methods were challenged, particularly the colonial mentality which had dominated the Victorian world-view. One striking speech by an Indian delegate has resonated down the century since that Conference. V.S. Azariah, who became Bishop of Dornakal, was invited to speak on "Co-operation between foreign and native workers in younger churches." One transcript of his words is as follows: *"I do not plead for returning calls, handshakes, chairs, dinners and teas as such. I do on the other hand plead for all of them and more if they can be expressions of a friendly feeling, if these or anything else can be the outward proofs of a real willingness on the part of the foreign missionary to show that he is in the midst of the people to be to them not a lord and master but a brother and a friend. Through all the ages to come the Indian Church will rise up in gratitude to attest the heroism and self denying labours of the missionary body. You have given your goods to feed the poor. You have given your bodies to be burned. We ask for love. Give us friends."*[3]

This quotation is relevant to Constance's years of preparation for missionary service because she was deeply convinced that she was sent out to be a true friend to the people she would serve. She was not at all happy about the colonial structures and overtones which she encountered in the early years of her service in Uganda. In her first letter after leaving Buganda for the wilds of Kigezi she wrote, *"It is a great change from the work I left at Namirembe amongst the Baganda, among whom I had in one place or another spent 6 years. I felt leaving them very much; nevertheless I quite knew it was time. I at least went to the heathen. The cry for 'more education, higher education' I realised I could not cope with. My friends whom I have left behind, had got to the stage when, if you went to see them, you 'called' and were given afternoon tea! The girls had become very independent, many had bicycles and dresses which my allowance would certainly not reach to: but I truly loved them, they were clean and had polished manners."* (November 1923). Some time in her missionary training or in the churches she attended, she must have absorbed the same sentiments as those which inspired V.S. Azariah of South India in 1910.

Application to the Church Missionary Society

In 1914 when Constance applied to the C.M.S., her elder sister, Lucy Mary, by this time had trained as a teacher and was all set to go out to a large girls' school in South Africa. Constance's surviving younger sister, whose name we do not know yet, had hopes of training as a nurse. It seems that only Constance herself did not go for a formal training for any recognised career. This is very surprising, given her prowess in Education in Uganda in later life. The heading of the article of the *Uganda Argus* quoted on pages 28 and 29 is, *"Miss Hornby, Kigezi Girls' No. 1 Teacher."* Up to the time she entered C.M.S. Training, she had no paper qualifications. On the Application Form to the Society one question was: "What examinations, degrees and diplomas do you hold?" In the middle of the large space below she wrote, *"I have never taken any examinations."* However, she was quite a well-educated young

---

[3]   Quoted from an archive which was published on the Internet by the India Missions Association in preparation for the Edinburgh 2010 Missionary Conference.

woman with a strong sense of duty, varied experience and many natural abilities. We could say that at the age of 30 in 1914 she was a graduate of the University of Life, a hard and very demanding school. Whatever she did or achieved in the future would be by the grace of God, and all glory should go to him.

How the C.M.S. trained future missionaries

The Church Missionary Society was founded on a strong Biblical foundation on April 12th 1799. The five missionary principles of John Venn were adopted, see below, and Constance as a missionary recruit would have studied and adopted these as her own. They shaped her later life.

The Five Missionary Principles of John Venn, 1799

1. Follow God's leading.
2. Begin on a small scale.
3. Put money in the second place, not the first.
4. Under God, all will depend on the type of men (and women) sent forth. A missionary should have heaven in his heart and tread the world under his foot.
5. Look for success only from the Spirit of God.

Source: Stock, Eugene (1898) One Hundred Years, being the Short History of the C.M.S., *pub. C.M.S., Salisbury Square, London.*

The Society placed much emphasis on the selection and training of its workers. The *Church Missionary Intelligencer* magazine of 1898 contains an illuminating article on "The Training of Women Missionaries" by G.A. Gollock. *"Spiritual men and women are needed for spiritual work"*, he wrote, and *"Training work should be full of wise individualism."* Residential training was essential to promote character development through the interplay of different personalities engaged in practical work in the House. He said, *"A spirit of Christian gladness and fellowship will prevail in the House."* There would be lectures and Bible studies coupled with learning about the Society and its work. Candidates would visit C.M. House at 6 Salisbury Square in the heart of the City of London and spend time individually with members of the Candidates' Committee.

It is interesting that all these features of training still prevailed at Foxbury, the post-World War II C.M.S. Women's Missionary Training College, in the 1960s. It can be assumed that the training which Constance received in 1914-1915 followed the same pattern. Other missionary societies at the time also shared the same methods, for example the China Inland Mission, as described in Mildred Cable and Francesca French's book *Ambassadors for Christ* (1935). Those two ladies were roughly contemporaries of Constance; they worked in Western China and the Gobi Desert doing pioneer evangelism. A comparative study of these three brave single ladies would be an interesting piece of research.

Missionary training college

Constance passed through the rigorous selection process early in 1914 and was sent to the Mildmay Training House named "The Willows" in Stoke Newington, north London. The C.M.S. did not have its own women's training college at that time and so candidates were sent to establishments run by other Missions. The men were trained nearby in Islington at the C.M.S. College founded in 1825. Women were moved to offer themselves to the Society during the Great Spiritual Awakening in the 1860s, but they were declined and Stock notes rather piously (p. 97) *"the time was not yet for 'Phebe' to go abroad on any large scale."* The first English women to go and work in Uganda arrived in 1895.

The Superintendent of "The Willows" was Miss M.D. Wood. She watched over Constance for four terms, seeing her grow into *"a steady-going, purposeful worker, gifted with sanctified commonsense . . . always considerate and thoughtful for others. Her strong point is evangelistic work, her brightness attracts the people and she gives her message with earnest simplicity and straightforwardness. She has proved the power of prayer in her own life."* (March 5th, 1915)

The Vicar of Paddington, Rev. E. Gross Hodge wrote a letter on 25th May 1915 recommending that she should be sent out in the autumn. He mentioned *"her winning personality . . . experience in devotion and the completeness of her surrender to Christ."* He further said, *"Her sense of duty is strong. It will give her stability and perseverance."* Constance was accepted as a missionary of C.M.S. in July 1915 for service in Africa but no further details could be given because the First World War (1914-18) was raging. The seas were very dangerous and the Society could not designate her to a country or fix a date for sailing. Constance was left "in limbo". She went home to her parents in Twickenham. She did not wish to be a burden to the Society during the straitened times of the War and so she wrote to the Secretary on 20th May 1915, *"In the event of the Society not being able to send me out this autumn, I should like them to know, I shall not require any money from them."*

Practical training as a midwife

At this juncture, her resourcefulness caused her to take action. She wrote a letter to the Society on 11th November 1915 saying, *"I was wondering how I could best use the time to be better fitted for the work. Would a short course of Midwifery or Dispensing be useful or would it be better to try one of the Military Hospitals and get a very general idea of the work?"* It was decided to send her to the Zenana Midwifery Training School, but the problem was finance. Constance wrote again, *"Father said I was to let you know, he will pay half; of course if the Society cannot give any help then I must find the rest. I just hate asking for money, which I feel I have not in the least earned; especially when I think how it is collected, but I fear I must."* (November 20th 1915) The Society granted £10 towards the fees and Constance began the training on January 17th 1916 in the Mildmay Hospital and went out visiting patients in their homes a month later. She told the reporter from the *Uganda Argus* (August 25th 1969) that she was posted as a certificated midwife to one of the poorest districts of London. *"Work was terribly difficult during the war. All doctors were very busy and I was left in charge of a hospital alone."* This training was part of God's plan and throughout her life in Uganda she tried to meet whatever need she saw, whether in health, education or in practical methods of solving problems. In 1941 when she handed over the girls' school in Kabale to a fully trained teacher, Miss Lilian Clark, she immediately offered to fill a gap as a Midwife in the Mission Hospital for six months and wrote to her supporters, *"I got my certificate while I was waiting to come out because of the last war, to mark time, and it has been most useful to me. I remember how I did not want to take it, but I passed, and did a job of work in England and then out here. We had 40 cases this year . . . "* (29th September, 1941)

Sailing to Uganda in 1916 during the First World War

Months passed, but the way became clearer. *"Trust in the Lord with all your heart, and lean not to your own understanding. In all your ways acknowledge him, and he will direct your paths."* (Proverbs 3 v. 5-6) A very welcome letter came from the C.M.S. dated June 17th 1916 allocating Constance to the Uganda Mission. She told the *Uganda Argus* reporter, *"I really feared going at first, although I had insisted on going there. One reason was that some of the missionaries who had been in Uganda had written about the martyrs and I knew I was no saint."* In October she sailed for East Africa. It must have been a perilous journey, but we have no information about it. She landed at Mombasa with her luggage and took the train on the "Uganda Railway" as far as Kisumu (Port Florence), then the steamer on Lake Victoria to Port Bell in Uganda. Thence she proceeded to Busoga, east of Kampala, where she began to work as both a teacher and a nurse at Iganga. Actually, the Busoga Railway was opened in 1912 but it stopped short of the River Nile, which was first bridged by the railway in 1931. The background to her assignment needs to be further explained; the future lay in God's hands.

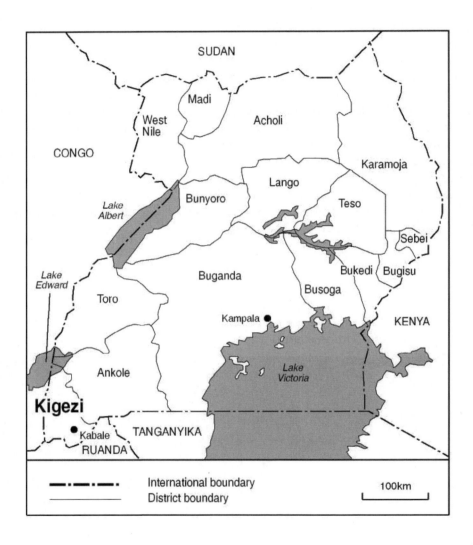

MAP OF UGANDA SHOWING DISTRICTS UNDER THE
BRITISH PROTECTORATE ADMINISTRATION

[REPRODUCED BY PERMISSION OF DR GRACE CARSWELL, UNIVERSITY OF SUSSEX]

Chapter Three

1916 – 1922
YEARS OF FAITHFUL SERVICE IN OBSCURITY

How the C.M.S. work in Uganda started

A salient point in the early history of mission work in Uganda was the letter which the explorer Henry M. Stanley wrote to the *Daily Telegraph* (14th April 1875): *"But oh! That some pious practical missionary would come here! What a field and harvest ripe for the sickle of civilisation! It is not the mere preacher, however that is wanted here . . . It is the practical Christian tutor, who can teach people to become Christians, cure their diseases, construct dwellings, understand and exemplify agriculture and turn his hand to anything, like a sailor – this is the man who is wanted."* Later in his book Stanley described the rich green landscape of Buganda and said of Kabaka Mutesa that he owned *"a land worth loving."*[1]

Only two days after the publication of Stanley's letter, an anonymous donation of £5,000 arrived at the Church Missionary Society (C.M.S.) Headquarters specifically designated for the Uganda Mission. The Society responded to the call by sending out eight men. Two of them, Wilson and Shergold Smith, reached Uganda in June 1877. Alexander Mackay joined them a year later. He was the son of a Scottish farmer from Rhynie in Aberdeenshire and had many practical skills as well as spiritual gifts. He was the "all rounder" who fitted Stanley's vision and it could be said that Constance Hornby was in the same mould. It is well known that both the Anglican Church and the Roman Catholic Church in Uganda suffered persecution in their early years. There were many martyrs, young Christian "readers" dying together for their faith at the cruel hand of Kabaka Mwanga, 1885-86. In October 1885 the first Bishop of Uganda, Bishop Hannington, on his way to Kampala

to begin his ministry, was brutally murdered in Busoga. This was

[1] See *Through the Dark Continent* Vol. I.

the District lying East of Kampala where Constance Hornby began her work only 30 years later.

Despite, or perhaps because of the opposition, the Church of Uganda grew. "The blood of the martyrs is the seed of the Church." It needed organisation and structure and this became the prime task of Bishop Alfred R. Tucker from 1890 until 1911. He followed the Principles of Henry Venn, a founding figure of C.M.S.: A Church should be *SELF-GOVERNING, SELF-SUPPORTING AND SELF-EXTENDING*. Evangelism was a strong feature of the Church of Uganda and the Gospel spread far and wide. Medical work was another pillar of the Church. Dr Albert Cook with his wife and other C.M.S. missionaries founded Mengo Hospital in Kampala in May 1897 and engaged in outreach work. In 1902-08 there was a terrible epidemic of Sleeping Sickness around the shores of Lake Victoria, causing the death of 200,000 people, particularly in Busoga where wide tracts of land had to be forcibly depopulated to stop the epidemic. Uganda was a disease-ridden country.

Constance Hornby's first assignment

The Protectorate Government from its declaration in 1894 struggled with administration and development at every level. Education was seen as a key factor. Missionary societies, Catholic and Protestant, laid the foundations and the Government willingly gave grants to mission schools and supervised the curriculum and standards. The Iganga Girls' Boarding School to which Constance was posted was founded by the C.M.S. and aided by the Government. Her job there was teaching and nursing combined. Sadly, after only a short time she became very ill with one of the worst diseases in Uganda, Black Water Fever. It was spread by mosquitoes and was a severe form of Malaria. Few people survived a bout, but Constance's strong constitution and prayers brought her through.

It is interesting to note that Constance was one of the seven young lady missionaries who were the predecessors of the later famous Florence Allshorn who went to Iganga Girls' School in 1920.[2] The

---

[2] See J.H. Oldham, p. 28, 32 and 35. He suggests that each of these young women only stayed for a short time, some leaving because of illness, others because they could not live at close quarters with the overbearing senior missionary.

influence and writings of Florence Allshorn are so well known in mission circles that it is appropriate to give a summary here. Constance never mentioned in her extant letters the relationship problem which Florence encountered in sharing accommodation with the senior missionary, who had a difficult personality. Florence did not have the benefit of Constance's missionary training, but she persevered under the yoke for four years and learned how to respond with Christian love instead of reacting bitterly to provocation. She read St Paul's teaching on love in I Corinthians chapter 13 every day for a year and sought to put it into practice. This experience shaped her views on the training of women missionaries. She became the Principal of the C.M.S. Training College and exerted great influence over many years, teaching inter-personal relationships as the core for successful missionary work. She did not return to Uganda until she made a visit shortly before her death in 1950. Although there is no record of any dialogue between them, Constance read widely and would have known about Florence and her later career from C.M.S. literature.

At Gayaza High School

Busoga must have been deemed too unhealthy for Constance and so she was re-located to Gayaza High School, north of Kampala. This school was founded by C.M.S. in 1905 and became the leading girls' school in the country. It was a good model for Constance to follow when she later pioneered girls' education in Kigezi District. The school uniform *"at first was a suuka, a cloth tied under the armpits and held up by a sash, leaving the shoulders bare; but Miss Allen designed a round-necked top for it with short Magyar sleeves."*[3] Apparently, the tailor at Gayaza, named Mr Gomez, developed the *Busuuti* from the design of the uniform and it became the national dress of Ugandan women. It is sometimes called *"Boodinge"* (from "uniform at a boarding school"), *"Gayaza"* or *"Gomesi"*. It is still very popular today and people may not know its origins.

Constance joined the staff in 1917 at the age of 33 and stayed there two years. Dr Algie Stanley Smith recalled that time with a comment on her youthful appearance, *"It was there I first met her.*

---

[3] *Gayaza High School 1905-1995* page 3.

There had been a severe epidemic of Small Pox all over Buganda, and I used to go regularly from Mengo Hospital to see the girls in the isolation camp we arranged for them, and I found a bright cheery young girl with her rosy cheeks, living with and caring for the sick girls."[4] In 1919, she succumbed again to the dreaded Black Water Fever. This time, she was sent back home to England for treatment and convalescence. We were told that she built up her strength at home by eating good plain food like milk and eggs. It is very unusual for a person to survive two attacks of Black Water Fever but she recovered and was allowed to sail back to East Africa.

At Mengo Hospital

In 1920, Constance aged 36 joined the staff of Mengo Hospital and worked as a midwife. In Sir Albert Cook's fascinating *Uganda Memories 1897-1940,* he tells of his own walk from the Coast in 1896-97: 800 miles with 200 porters and 46 brown donkeys. At least, Constance Hornby had the benefit of the Uganda Railway as far as Kisumu and then a Lake Steamer to reach the heart of Uganda whenever she needed to travel to and from Mombasa. After founding Mengo Hospital with his wife as Matron, Dr Cook perceived the need to train midwives. Together they planned a Midwifery Training School (M.T.S.) where young women of any religious background (Catholic, Protestant, Moslem or Hindu) would be welcome. It was to serve all sections of the population. The Governor of Uganda and Lady Coryndon gave it their enthusiastic support. Thus it was named after her when it opened in June 1921 with Mrs A.R. Cook as the Lady Superintendent. Then, in July, Dr Cook and his wife decided to go on a long medical safari which they called a "Social Purity" campaign, going round all the main centres of population in Uganda. What to do about the M.T.S. in Mrs Cook's absence? Constance Hornby to the rescue! With some sense of relief Dr Cook mentions that they left the Training School in her capable hands. What a stalwart person she was proving to be.

Link with the Girls' Friendly Society

The years after the First World War were very hard economically. In the 1920s Europe sunk into the Great Depression when there was high unemployment, inflation and widespread poverty. Inevitably, the

---

[4]   Quoted from Dr Algie Stanley Smith's address at Miss Hornby's funeral.

Churches were affected and the levels of giving to overseas missionary work fell. Constance Hornby had straitened circumstances and must have prayed a lot about the support for her work. In a remarkable way, God prepared a channel through which the backing for her pioneering work in Kigezi could be supplied. The next part of the story is based on findings in the Archives of the Girls' Friendly Society (G.F.S.).

While serving at Mengo Hospital, Constance met Miss Elsie Cook, the niece of Dr Albert Cook. She was a trained Pharmacist and a C.M.S. missionary. Part of her support came from the Girls' Friendly Society, of which she was "Our Own Missionary" in Uganda. After Constance left Mengo Hospital in 1923 to go to Kigezi, Elsie Cook became engaged to be married to Mr J.F. Robinson, a teacher at King's College, Budo, and she resigned from the G.F.S. In 1925, Constance was invited to become the next "Our Own Missionary" in Uganda and the Society played a major role in her life and work for more than twenty years.

The G.F.S. was a large uniformed organisation in England catering for Christian young women of a more senior age-range than the Girl Guides or Girls' Brigade. It had hundreds of Branches in Churches scattered all over the country. Members were mostly working women and they enjoyed meeting together in free time for practical instruction, such as needlework and craft work, fellowship and Bible teaching. They had their own magazine with stories, competitions and news from overseas. They made children's clothes, dolls and other items to send out in parcels to their Own Missionaries. They also raised funds to support them. The G.F.S. Uganda Mission Fund was started in 1921 when they collected exactly £39 10s 3d to send to C.M.S. towards the support of Miss Elsie Cook. The ethos of the G.F.S. appears to be altruistic Christian patriotism. Here is an extract from the Minutes of the Overseas Empire Education Committee (1927-31): They quoted the Archbishop of Canterbury's words, "*Plainly the Christian citizen is bound to regard the Empire as a trust which we hold, not for the gratification of pride or for the accumulation of wealth, but for the benefit of its peoples and of all the world.*" They said, "*These words are a call to every member of the G.F.S. to show herself worthy of that trust. We believe that the British Empire has one of the biggest contributions to make towards the good of mankind.*" They resolved that their watch-words should be, "*Responsibility, Duty, Sympathy and Self Sacrifice.*"

The actual plaque which belonged to Miss Hornby. [*Photographed by E. Traill 2009, with permission from the Girls' School Headmistress*]

There are many references to the G.F.S. in Miss Hornby's letters from Kigezi. She attributed much of her pioneering work to their prayers and support. Her discipline and diligence in writing regular letters with vivid descriptions of her work all through the years until her retirement were probably due to her sense of duty and dedication to the G.F.S. as the supporting agency both of her own ministry and of the Kabale Girls' School. There is a sheaf of her letters from 1923 onwards when she went to Kabale, gleaned from the G.F.S. magazines and from *Ruanda Notes*.[5]

Theological Dissent

Another aspect of the 1920s was the theological debate between the "Liberals" and the "Evangelicals". When Dr Len Sharp and Dr Algie Stanley Smith, who were young doctors at Mengo Hospital, heard God's call to the area known as "Ruanda" bordering the south-west corner of Uganda they found themselves without the full support of the wider Church Missionary Society because of their Biblical position. The story of the founding of the "Ruanda Mission" is well documented elsewhere. To our knowledge, Constance Hornby never mentioned the controversy in her letters to supporters. She was a practical Christian missionary, totally devoted to serving her Master and helping his people. Her own personal faith was founded on her reading of the Scriptures and her experience of answered prayer. She lived in harmony with the members of the C.M.S. in the Uganda Mission but had no great difficulty in fitting into the new

---

5   The magazine of the Ruanda Mission, C.M.S.

6   The plaque is kept safely by the Head Teacher of Bishop Kivengere Girls' School, Muyebe.

"Ruanda Mission". At some stage in her life, it may have been at that time, she took a piece of plywood the size of a large book and stippled the word *"RABBONI"* on it with a red hot poker. In one translation of John 20 v. 16, it means *"MY GREAT MASTER"*, the answer of Mary Magdalene to Jesus when he appeared to her, risen and alive for evermore and called her by name. Constance hung this simple plaque[6] on the wall of her room.

It was amongst her few worldly possessions when she died in 1972 and seems to have been her special text. The sight of it made a deep impression on those who visited her in her little house on Rugarama Hill toward the end of her life.

The little known district of Kigezi

RWENTOBO HILL: THE ENTRANCE TO KIGEZI DISTRICT. *[E. TRAILL 2010]*

Meanwhile, when Dr and Mrs Cook were on their travels in 1921 they visited Kigezi District in the South-West of Uganda. In his Journal, he describes their journey by motor car along the 93-mile road from Mbarara to Kabale. Many were the hazards, including broken bridges, but they persevered and came to the massive mountain named Rwentobo Hill where the plains of Ankole are broken by the upthrust of the dissected plateau of Kigezi.

He writes, *"The road had been ascending steadily for some miles and the water was boiling furiously in the radiator, so we stopped to cool the engine and have lunch. They had a pleasant custom here of sending a crowd of Bakiga to help motors up the otherwise impossibly steep hill. My wife and I walked most of the way up the hill (to lighten the car) with a few men shoving behind, then we hitched on the fifty men, and they hauled the car up the extremely steep gradient of the last five hundred yards. The District Commissioner had kindly wired, bidding us go slowly at the hairpin bends, and these indeed were many and exceedingly sharp . . . With numerous stops on the hills, we got to the Government station at Kabale by sunset, only two miles from our destination, but in descending the last hill the rim of one of the hind wheels came right off, shearing off nuts and lugs. We could not find the latter anywhere, but help was at hand, for Dr Sharp and Dr Stanley Smith had come out to meet us, and in the gathering dusk we jacked up the car, and lashed the rim and tyre on with rope. We had the kindest welcome and a hot tea in front of a blazing fire at Dr and Mrs Stanley Smith's which we appreciated the more for not having had time to make tea on the road."* (September 14th, 1921)

The Uganda Mission based in Kampala under the leadership of Bishop Willis was concerned about the wild south-west extremity of the country known as Kigezi District. It had been brought under the Protectorate Administration in 1911-12. There had been a rebellion there against British rule which will be described later. The leadership of the young Church of Uganda proposed the evangelisation of Kigezi. Some "Black Evangelists" (see Louise Pirouet's study) worked there with varying results: one named Zakaria Balaba was speared to death in the Kisoro area. Small churches were founded but there was a great need both for settled Administration and well organised medical, educational and pastoral development.

Pioneer medical missionaries

In the 1920s, in answer to many prayers, two young missionary doctors, Dr Len Sharp and Dr Algie Stanley-Smith, with their wives became the pioneers of Christian medical work and much else besides. The doctors had been in military service in the First World War and were posted to Mengo Hospital following the invitation of Dr Albert Cook. It was for a time a base hospital for the East African

Campaign. The doctors had been close friends since student days at Cambridge University and had heard God's clear call to the territory of Ruanda-Urundi which borders the South-West corner of Uganda. The story of how God overruled political circumstances is fully told in other books (see Bibliography.) The way into the unevangelised and medically needy territory of Ruanda-Urundi was not fully open until a few years later but the doctors decided to start medical mission work based at Kabale, the administrative headquarters of Kigezi District, as a first step towards Ruanda-Urundi. They had the encouragement of Dr Albert Cook and Bishop Willis of Uganda. The C.M.S. approved the setting up of the *Ruanda Mission* within the larger Society, but with its own doctrinal basis, as a venture of faith and obedience to God's call.

The doctors set out

A nursing sister at Mengo Hospital, Constance Watney, offered to join the doctors. On 4th February 1921 *"Dr and Mrs Len Sharp left Kampala on a motorcycle – Mrs Sharp ('quite terrified of going into the unknown' as she remembered later) riding pillion, with their baggage and some medical equipment following them in a van. The road to Mbarara was familiar to Len, and after the journey of 170 miles on rough murram roads, they were welcomed by the Rev and Mrs Harold Lewin, the missionaries in the C.M.S. centre at Mbarara. The next two weeks were spent in recruiting about 100 porters to carry their belongings, since vehicles could go no further at that time, and making arrangements for the next stage of their journey."* With them were some faithful Ugandan co-workers to organise the porters. It was quite a trek. They reached Kabale on 24th February and went to the Government hill for information. Esther Sharp took up the story, *"When my husband and I arrived at the Government centre of Kabale on 24th February, we found a very primitive little place. Our mission hill was pointed out to us across the valley and very bare it looked too. It was raining and the motor bike on which we had travelled had to be left at the bottom of the hill as we toiled up the slippery path, often literally on our knees."*[7] The vivid, first-hand account of the arrival of the party at Kabira Station, Rugarama Hill, Kabale, makes exciting reading. Dr and Mrs Algie Stanley Smith with baby Nora followed by stages in due course.

---

[7] Quoted from Makower, p. 48.

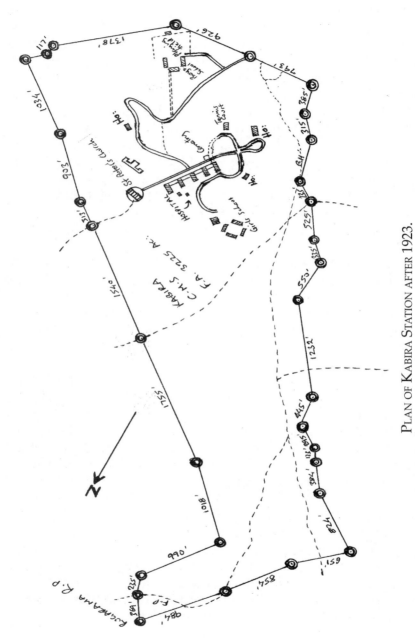

PLAN OF KABIRA STATION AFTER 1923.

[*TRACED BY PHILIP TIBENDERANA BY PERMISSION OF THE DIOCESAN SECRETARY, KIGEZI*]

First Church building on Rugarama Hill, 1921.
[Drawing from Ruanda Notes, C.M.S. Archives]

Kabira Station in 1923 showing the first hospital (left), and the
first school (top right). *[From Ruanda Notes, C.M.S. Archives]*

Building Kabira mission station

They set about planning and laying out an access road and one straight up the ridge of the spur called Rugarama Hill, which juts out into the wide valley at Kabale. Their plan has been preserved in the office of the Diocese of Kigezi. They employed large numbers of labourers (200 at one time) for road-building, also building workers and carpenters. They put up simple but commodious thatched houses for themselves and laid plans for Kigezi Hospital on the site now occupied by Kigezi High School (Secondary) on Rugarama Hill. This formed Kabira Station. They had found a small Church on the hill, planted by the evangelists from Ankole and Toro. The Government was also proceeding with road-building from Mbarara to Kabale, so that by the time of Dr and Mrs Cook's visit in September 1921 a motor car could get through with difficulty. By that time, the two doctors were fairly well settled.

It was a time of very hard work physically, with many dangers by day and hungry leopards prowling at night, but as in the book of Nehemiah, prayer and work went on hand in hand and *"The joy of the Lord is your strength."*[8] Dr Len Sharp was appointed part-time District Medical Officer for Kigezi, initially using two buildings on the Government Hill approximately a mile away as his "hospital", with a Muganda fellow-worker called Erisa Mutiaba in charge, until the hospital on Rugarama Hill was completed. This was a sign of the warm support and approval of the Protectorate Government. Faithful staff for the medical work was gathered into a team under Constance Watney as Matron. Sadly, she fell sick herself in mid-1922 soon after the new Kigezi Hospital began to admit patients and she had to return to England leaving a big gap.

Early educational work

The doctors also pioneered educational work. In June 1921 they founded Kisoro High School at Seseme which was later transferred to Kabale and became Kigezi High School on Rugarama Hill in February 1922.[9]

---

[8] Nehemiah 8 v. 10.

[9] Quoting from the Kigezi High School Golden Jubilee booklet 1972, "In February 1922 (actually the two-dominated date of 2-2-22), the School was opened by the Provincial Commissioner, Mr P. Cooper . . . The Headmaster was Mr Samwiri Sebuliba, a young Muganda . . . Dr Stanley Smith recalls 'Eleven little boys, who arrived clad in skins, each trailing a goat, which was the original admission fee.' Later in the year the number increased to 24."

They aimed to educate and train the sons of chiefs and leaders, while sharing the life-changing Gospel of Jesus Christ with them. They desired to extend education to women and girls, but there was considerable resistance. Mrs Esther Sharp and Mrs Zoe Stanley Smith, aided by little Nora, did all they could to gather them together. Dr Algie began a letter to supporters in June 1923 thus, *"My wife and I went for a three weeks' safari through Rukiga in April accompanied by our little Nora aged 3. We found signs nearly everywhere of a marked progress in the gospel, and 7 more new centres were either opened up or prospected, where the light of the knowledge of Jesus Christ will illumine the gloom of heathen darkness. My wife and Nora proved a lodestar of attraction to the women and girls. In nearly every centre they number less than 10% of the adherents, and it needs the presence of a lady and the winsomeness of a little child to break down the walls of prejudice and fear which keep them from coming to Jesus. Nora played her part nobly: as she went along the road in her carrying basket, shouting her greetings to them, and as she sat in her tent with her simple toys around her they responded to her innocence and once again 'a little child did lead them.'"*

Constance Hornby sent to Kigezi

The dual need of a Matron to replace Constance Watney and the opening mission work amongst women and girls was communicated to praying friends at Mengo Hospital. God's call came clearly to two single ladies, Beatrice Martin who was a nurse and Constance Hornby at the Midwifery Training School. They responded and the Hospital released them. Dr Sharp travelled on his motor-bike with side car to Kampala to collect them. They made the two-day journey to Kabale in March 1923. Mrs Esther Sharp described it, *"After an adventurous journey over the primitive roads of those days and largely in the dark (by candlelight as the acetylene lamp had failed), they arrived safely, together with the first grey Persian kitten to venture into these parts."*[10]

For Constance, this was the beginning of her true life's work, the one for which God had shaped her. She was in her 39th year and had a wealth of experience, a deep commitment to her Lord and Master, a lively mind and a good sense of humour, a combination which could be called "sanctified common sense". Kigezi would become her home, the Bakiga her people. She would be loved and accepted and also changed by them as they shared in the knowledge of God and worked together.

---

[10] Extract from article in the *Uganda Church Review 1954-55, Winter Quarter.*

MAP OF KIGEZI SHOWING SAZAS (COUNTIES).

[REPRODUCED BY PERMISSION OF DR GRACE CARSWELL, UNIVERSITY OF SUSSEX]

Chapter Four
1923 – 1930
PIONEERING FOR CHRIST IN KIGEZI DISTRICT

The Land and its People

Kigezi in the twenty-first century is known as the "Switzerland of Africa" for its tourist potential. It is an ancient upland area, contorted rocks bearing witness to earth movements and millennia of cycles of erosion. It is a dissected plateau, the rounded mountain tops being remarkably at the same altitude (about 7,000ft or 2,134m) and aligned in parallel ridges with wide swamp-filled valleys between. It borders the edge of the western branch of the Great Rift Valley which is a massive cleft in the Earth's surface stretching from the Jordan Valley in the north to the lower Zambezi Valley. There is a range of towering volcanoes and numerous smaller cones associated with the Rift Valley in Kigezi where it borders with Rwanda and Congo. The area is subject to occasional earthquakes. It is on the watershed between the Nile and Congo Basins. Tourists now enjoy visiting Lake Bunyonyi, one of the deepest lakes in Africa, also the waterfalls, hot springs and other interesting features. The Mountain Gorilla has two reserves in Kigezi and a part of the Queen Elizabeth National Park is included in this beautiful district. Kabale, the chief town, is less than 2 degrees south of the Equator, but is at an altitude of 6,000ft/1,829m and so the climate is a cool version of the typical Equatorial pattern. This means that there are two rainy seasons around the Equinoxes in March and September and two dry seasons between. Most of Kigezi receives ample rainfall for almost continuous cultivation of crops. In the 21st century it is one of the most densely populated parts of rural Africa, and also one of the poorest.

However, in the early 1920s the District had only recently (1912) been demarcated for inclusion within the British administration of the Uganda Protectorate. Little was known about it and development of roads and services was only beginning. There is a touch of the explorer in the writings of the early missionaries, particularly Dr Len Sharp and Dr Algie Stanley Smith. Access was difficult because the parallel ridges of mountains lay at right angles to the main route south-westwards from Kampala. Rwentobo Hill is a long ridge forming a formidable obstacle at the boundary of Kigezi with the flatter plains of Ankole. It is described by Dr Algie in 1921: *"We are set on the summit of Africa. I wish I could draw you an adequate pen picture of the beauty of this place. In coming here one toils up a great hill 1,000ft or more and finds oneself transported away from the hot steamy plains of Ankole up into a spacious upland country of piled-up hills and deep-cut valleys, and everywhere the signs of cultivation. These industrious people, who live mostly down in the depths of the valleys, carry their cultivation way up to the mountain tops, sometimes 1,500ft above, and here at Kabale, through a gap in the hills we can see the great extinct volcano Muhavura, one of the finest peaks of the Mufumbiro range."*[1]

One of the many "Hornby stories" related to us tells how Miss Hornby with a new missionary, possibly Beatrice Martin in 1923, was climbing Rwentobo Hill on foot. The newcomer collapsed with fatigue saying, "I think I'm going to die!" Miss Hornby urged her on saying, "You can't do that yet, you have work to do!" Pioneers had to be tough and determined. Disease and ignorance were rampant. Early photographs in Carswell's book reveal that most of the hills were fairly bare with few trees (not eucalyptus, which was introduced later). Strip cultivation was practised along the contours with ridges formed by piling up stones and weeds on the hills, a forerunner of formal terracing. Cultivation was women's work with simple hoes and a few other tools. The staple crops were peas, beans, millet, sorghum and sweet potatoes. The Bakiga produced surplus food crops which they traded for salt from Lake Katwe.[2] They kept some animals, small cattle, sheep and goats, also chickens. The livestock were kept for trade or for marriage arrangements. Leopards ranged around at night preying on the livestock.[3] The missionaries had to be multi-skilled in order to survive and to pioneer in their different fields, church-planting, medical work and education.

---

[1] Quoted from Makower, p. 54-55.

[2] Lake Katwe is a small volcanic lake adjacent to Lake Edward in the Rift Valley. It is a source of rock salt. The trade routes for this valuable resource traditionally crossed Kigezi going to Ruanda and Congo (see Carswell *Cultivating Success in Uganda*, 2007).

[3] According to the Uganda National Parks Handbook (1971), "The LEOPARD (*panthera pardus*), which is seldom abroad during daylight, is not often seen. A well-grown male leopard can weigh as much as 70 kilograms, but is usually much less; it measures about 2.25 metres from nose to the tip of its

LEOPARD HUNTING AT NIGHT. *[PHOTO ROGER F.L. WILKINS, TAKEN IN KRUGER NATIONAL PARK, R.S.A.]*

The Religion of the Bakiga before Christian missionaries arrived

The Bakiga people were organised in clans and traditionally had no king or other supreme ruler. Spiritually, until the coming of the African evangelists and the missionaries from outside, they followed traditional religious beliefs. Canon Peter Rwabyoma explains, *"They shared a trait common to their neighbours: Bafumbira and Bahororo. This trait is also exhibited by nearly all the Africans. It is about being notoriously religious."* He quotes from Professor John S. Mbiti, a Kenyan clergyman, who wrote that, *"Africans are notoriously religious,"* and that *"religion permeates every department of life."*[4] He goes on to quote what he considers to be the

---

tail. The markings on a leopard's coat take the form of spots and rosettes, which blend into an indefinite grey when the animal is seen at a distance. Leopards are solitary by habit, and hunt mostly at night when they kill birds, small to medium-sized antelopes, and animals of many other kinds. They are active climbers and often take their prey up into trees to eat it undisturbed by scavengers."

[4] John S. Mbiti, *African Religions and Philosophy*, Heinemann, London 1969, p. 1.

most accurate description of the Bakiga and their religion, by Bishop Festo Kivengere, in the Introduction to Patricia St John's book *Breath of Life* (1971): *"In our religious life we were always striving to appease the distant, forbidding Creator from whom we sought desperately for security. The only possible relationship with this Creator seemed to be through the medium-spirits of our ancestors. We hoped that these would plead our cause, convince Him of our worthiness, and bring us the security for which we longed. This longing made our people redouble their efforts to find ways and means of appeasing the spirits but we never received the assurance we were seeking. We were haunted by a terrible sense of uncertainty."* Canon Peter says, *"The idea or the concept of God the Creator was not strange to the African Bakiga. They called Him 'Kazooba' – the one God who shone like the Sun. It was within such a religious atmosphere that the Good News of the Love of God reached the Bakiga in 1912. It was brought initially by the Baganda and Banyankole evangelists. Christian missionaries from Britain arrived among the Bakiga in 1921."*[5]

The Economic and Political Background

Economically and politically, in the early 1920s Kigezi was in a depressed state. An historian, F. Geraud W.F. throws light on the situation: *"The coming of the foreigners was the beginning of a new era for the Bakiga . . . What they saw was the result of 30 years of war . . . the outcome of almost 30 years of almost perpetual fighting, disturbances, plunder and raids from all sides. To these misfortunes were added the rinderpest and small-pox epidemics (1882 and 1892), the locust invasion, the famine of 1897 (Rwaranda) and the famine of 1904 (Mushorongo). During those years of great distress many things were wiped out. Even the deepest family ties were put under excessive stress. During that terrible time of the famine parents went as far as exchanging their children for a bit of food. What the foreigners saw, in arriving into Kigezi, was a decimated people in a desolated country . . . If the foreigners had come before 1875 . . . they would have found commercial routes (Katwe salt), traders and artistic expressions and they would have appreciated the agricultural skill and energy of the people of the mountains."* [6]

Another historian who later became a Member of the Uganda Parliament, E. Nathan Bisamunyu, identifies four main problems. First, local leadership was lacking. The Bakiga, being a conglomeration of

---

[5]   Canon Peter Rwabyoma at Bishop Barham University College, Paper, 2009.

[6]   In D. Denoon (ed.), *A History of Kigezi*, circa 1972, p. 53-54.

clans, did not appear to have any chiefs. D. Denoon adds, *"It would be fair to describe the Bakiga in 1900 as extravagantly decentralised politically."*[7] The first District Commissioners, who were all British, decided to appoint Baganda Agents to assist them. Generally they worked well, but some of these Agents proved to be corrupt and practised extortion, causing much ill feeling. The years of the First World War (1914-18) were not happy ones.

In 1919, a new District Commissioner, Captain J.E.T. Philips, decided to end the era of Baganda Agents. After a "trial and error" period with men from Bufumbira, which borders Rwanda, or from Tanzania (who caused the language used for administration to be changed to Swahili), he finally found some Bakiga elders with leadership potential. They were appointed as chiefs. These included Paulo Ngologoza (later Secretary General of Kigezi, 1946-55) who came to know Miss Hornby and appreciated her hard work. Captain Philips started a school in Bufumbira at Rusiiza (Gisoro) in 1920, where Swahili was taught. He wanted to start a school in Kabale. Next, as mentioned before, the C.M.S. doctors founded what became Kigezi High School at Seseme, near Kisoro in Bufumbira. Owing to local opposition, it was moved to Kabale in 1922. It began on Rugarama Hill but soon the school moved down to the valley, occupying the site of the present K.H.S. Primary. Education and leadership training were key concerns when Miss Hornby arrived in 1923. Her arrival was perfectly timed.

The second problem identified by Bisamunyu was the general poverty of the District. The population was always rising, but the steep hillsides and swampy valleys provided for only limited subsistence agriculture. There were no cash crops at first. The Baganda Agents introduced bananas to the warmer parts of Kigezi and they encouraged coffee growing. Black wattle trees were planted (to produce tannin, for leather), also hill rice and wheat. The British administrators found that vegetables grew well. These all helped the economy to some extent.

The other two problems were intertwined in Bisamunyu's view, namely drunkenness and Nyabingi troubles. Alcoholism might be viewed as the besetting sin of the Bakiga, based on home brewing. It was not until the time of the Revival in the 1930s that the hold of alcohol on most of the male population could be broken by the power of Christ.

---

[7]   *Ibid.* p. 213.

The related problem of the worship of evil spirits, the Nyabingi, caused even more trouble for the Administration. From about 1900 a lady named Muhumuza was the head or queen of the Nyabingi cult. She led a revolt which culminated in a battle in 1911 in the valley north-west of Kabale. The original Government Headquarters were at Ikumba (near present-day Hamurwa) and the Queen's camp was at Ihanga, now a market centre on the Kisoro road. In an armed struggle she was shot and arrested and her followers scattered. The rebellion petered out after she was exiled to Kampala, where she died in 1945. The destabilising influence of the Nyabingi went underground but re-emerged occasionally in subsequent years.

Heralds of new faiths from outside

As mentioned before, the first Protestant evangelists were from Buganda and they naturally worked in association with the Administrative Agents. Zakaria Balaba was the pioneer. According to Ngologoza[8] he built the first church at Kikungyere (present Kikungiri near Kabale) in 1912 but the District Commissioner advised him to move to Kabira (Rugarama Hill) in 1913. Sadly, Balaba was killed in Bufumbira on a preaching safari. He and other evangelists faithfully prepared the soil and sowed the good seed of God's Word. Rugarama Hill overlooking Kabale Town became the centre for the Anglican Church. A few miles away, south of Kabale, Rushoroza Hill was chosen by the Roman Catholics as the site of their first church, built by Yowana Kitagana in 1911. Like Balaba, he was a Muganda. Muslims also arrived in Kigezi to spread their faith. According to Ngologoza (p.69) the first mosque in Kigezi was built at Kirigime, near Kabale, by a teacher named Sharif.

When the first British C.M.S. missionaries arrived, a lot of development and many changes were in process. Roads were being constructed, using tax-labour. This was unpopular, as was the Government Poll Tax system which started in 1915. Money (Rupees) was introduced by the traders and the people had to exchange their cows or goats in order to pay the tax. The Rupee was the original currency of Uganda, used to pay the Indian labour on the Uganda Railway. In 1922 the East African Shilling was introduced and the Poll

---

[8]   *Kikezi and its Peoples*, p. 67, see Bibliography.

Tax was six shillings per person, used for the development of the District.

Miss Hornby's initial strategy

Miss Hornby arrived and began work amongst women and girls in March 1923. She recorded her impressions in her letters to the Ruanda Mission C.M.S. and the Girls' Friendly Society, which supported her. The task was enormous but she tackled it with energy and determination. She appears to have had three principles applying to the way she worked: *to identify with the people; to develop relationships; to proclaim the Good News of Jesus*. Like a rope, these three strands can be detected in her letters and throughout her life-story. For further reading on these principles, showing how they underpinned the ministry of our Lord on Earth, we recommend Dr Joe Aldrich's book *Lifestyle Evangelism* (see Bibliography). He writes, "*Christians are to be good news before they share the good news.*"(p.19) Miss Hornby's way was to live with her staff and girls, like her Master (ref. John 1 v. 14) who "*invited men to live with him 24 hours a day. His strategy was to become flesh and live among them. The term 'live among' could be translated 'to pitch a tent'. It is used in the Greek translation of the Old Testament to describe the tabernacle where God's presence 'lived among' them . . . Like the Old Testament tabernacle, Jesus became the shrine of his Father's glory. Is there any 'glory beheld' if there is no 'pitching among'?*" (p. 31)

The Beginnings of the Girls' School

In May 1923, Dr Len and Mrs Esther Sharp went with Miss Hornby to Bufumbira for a three week safari as a part of her orientation. They observed the fascinating geographical features of that volcanic area, and also the deep physical and spiritual needs of the people. He wrote, "*Miss Hornby returned richer than she went, for she was given four girls to form the nucleus of her future boarding school.*" (June 1923) The story of what happened during the night is well known. One of the girls, Miriam, told Canon Sam Mfitumukisa[9] how Miss Hornby tied a rope around their legs, her own leg and her safari box before sleeping. When the girls realised that she was in a deep slumber, they carefully untied the

---

[9] Extract from thesis "*The coming of Christianity to the Bufumbira area, 1912-1980*" by Canon Sam Mfitumukisa, 1987.

rope and walked back the 12 miles to Kisoro in the darkness. The next day, Miss Hornby returned to Bufumbira and managed to "re-arrest" the four girls, who had been duly chastised by their parents. Then, accompanied by their mothers, they had to walk the entire distance of 40 miles to Kabale in one day so that the four girls could not escape again.

First girls in Miss Hornby's School. *[Photo by Dr Len Sharp 1923, from the Archives, Bishop Barham University College]*

Dr Algie Stanley Smith also wrote in June 1923, "*Our work among the women and girls has been greatly strengthened by the coming of Miss Hornby . . . Grounds have been laid out for the Girls' School, and a schoolroom and dormitory will soon be put up. It is some indication of the financial straitness under which so much mission work is carried on today, that all the Uganda mission could spare for the starting of this work was £10. It is with the greatest thankfulness to God that we have received Miss Hornby in our midst, and we do specially ask for your prayers for her and for Miss Martin, who has come to take charge of the nursing work in the Hospital.*"

The Bakiga often give nicknames to incomers and quickly decided that *Nyakaishiki* (the young, unmarried girl) fitted Miss Hornby. According to Dr Manuel Muranga whose father was a boy during the 1920s, a rumour went around that Miss Hornby was looking for young people to take them away and eat them. Consequently, many boys and girls hid themselves in the bushes on the hillsides whenever they feared that the dreaded *Nyakaishiki* was coming. It was only the most foresighted Bakiga parents who had the courage to entrust their precious children to the care of the white missionaries. Future leaders, such as John Bikangaga and Festo Kivengere were among the few boys who were sent to school in the early years.[10] It was a considerable achievement that by November 1923, Miss Hornby had 20 girls in her school, drawn from Ruanda, Rukiga, Ankole and Buganda.[11]

How Miss Hornby approached her work

In her first letter to the Ruanda Mission, the three strands, identification (incarnation), relationships and proclamation, can all be found: *"This is the first time I have had the privilege of writing to you about this work. I started work here in March . . . After two days only on the road, I found here a crowd of women and girls clad in skins; and on that day in March, I wondered if I could ever get to know them; to love them seemed beyond the flight of imagination. But as usual my way was made easy; the people already trusted those who had started working here, their names round*

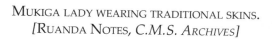

MUKIGA LADY WEARING TRADITIONAL SKINS.
[RUANDA NOTES, C.M.S. ARCHIVES]

---

[10] Manuel J.K. Muranga, Makerere University, paper *"Remembering Canon John Bikangaga soon after his death."* December 2006.

[11] For those who know Rugarama Hill today, her house still stands. It is now the one of the Boys' Houses of Kigezi High School. The Girls' School buildings were on the spur beyond the house, where the Boys' Dormitories now stand.

*about being a password . . . I truly believe that the women are past masters[12] in
'don't care-ishness' and rudeness as you visit. They won't at first even speak;
after a time they look up and grunt. "I have come to see you, my friend."
"Can't you see that I am working?" may be the reply. Then I just squat and go
on talking, and in many places now they are quite pleased to see me.*

*What a life these women and girls live, work, work, work nothing else! Off
with a baby on their back, a basket on their heads, huge hoe in one hand, a wee
piece of fire (a small piece of glowing wood in grass) in the other hand, they are
off to their food patch away on the top of some hill where they stay until nightfall,
when they return and cook for the men. Such is their life, and yet in spite of
this fact they won't try to save their girls from the same fate; 'It is good enough
for me, and was for my grandparents; why do you want to teach our girls? Let
them alone.' Sometimes I feel that if I could get the older women away, the
girls would come. However, when I tell the teachers, when to cheer one up they
say, 'Oh, you'll never get the girls to come and learn!' I say to them and to
myself, 'God is able, and they are His people, when all is said and done' even if
they have been left in darkness so long. And He has done wonderful things.*

*I am writing now in the new schoolroom, there are 20 girls all sitting on
the floor; it is the time for sewing class, and they are learning happily using an
odd bit of cloth which I have begged. All are here with the full consent of their
parents. Our wants, simple as they are, are supplied daily; we have no store,
but we live from day to day. One of my boxes holds all our worldly wealth.
Each girl has a blanket, a mat, a dress and a cloth for digging in. Everything
has come as a gift from someone and we have never been in need; but I need not
say of course that no fees or help come from these people as yet, for they are
very poor, they have just nothing.*

*By using girls in our house instead of boys as servants, 6 are supported.
I believe that 30 shillings would support a girl for a year at the present time. If
only one could better show what this people's need is, if only the world could
see what a change it makes in a girl when she is beginning to learn of Christ,
one would not need to speak.*

                    Yours sincerely,
                    C. Hornby"

This first letter gives a full impression of the situation she was in. Later,
after Leave in England, she revised her opinion of the attitude of the
women to her: *"I once said in my haste: 'All Bakiga are wonderfully*

---

[12] Past master: according to the Concise Oxford Dictionary, in this context, a
thorough master of a subject.

inhospitable,' and, as I slandered them in Ruanda Notes *I now wish to say that I am sorry. They don't know, bless them, what I said, but since I've been back I've had some of the best hospitality in the world . . ."* (March 14th, 1926) This was typical of Miss Hornby. She was a very straightforward lady who could speak quite sharply but who always apologised when she found she was mistaken. People began to sense the loving kindness which shone from her bright blue eyes and to love her as a person.

The school routine

In her next letter, she described the school: *"Just what to write I don't know, for every day seems alike. School from 8.30 – 12 and 1.30 – 4.15. I think a real educationalist would be not a little surprised at my school, for we number 20 now . . . At first only two girls could read at all and none could write or add. But now some, who have done wonderfully well, have learnt to read and write, and know the first three rules in Arithmetic. They all sew and do basketwork, and last but not least they dig and cook their own food."* She formed a strong bond with her girls and wanted the best for each one. *"Three of the girls are to be married this year, and the men have already paid the dowry for them. Two of the girls came to me and begged me to try to get the weddings put off for another six months; it was very hard for me to refuse, but I just dare not interfere. But when I see just happy school girls playing Rounders or Twos and Threes or skipping, I can but turn away and wish . . . Next year they will be women (aged about 17 not more)."* She made sure that the girls learned about Jesus and were prepared for Baptism. She gave an example, citing two of the girls, *"Both these girls are ready to be baptised as far as knowledge goes, but until now they have held back. But just now one has come and told me that she wants to be baptised and that she feels so happy. The other is still struggling with a quick temper, poor girl, which she can't control; she says it would be easier to cut off her hand than rule her tongue – and I believe her."* (Early 1924)

A protective strategy

One story from the early years of the school, unsupported by her letters but confirmed by Bishop William Rukirande[13] as being true to her character, is as follows. The first dormitory for the girls had a thatched roof and there was a gap above the walls below the thatch for ventilation

---

[13] Interview with Bishop William Rukirande, 31st December, 2010.

at night. Miss Hornby saw that an intruder could enter there and so she devised a clever strategy. She went to see the District Commissioner and the District Medical Officer and said that every one of her girls had a hoe under her bed and she had instructed them to wield their hoes against any man who might try to climb into the dormitory. She told the District Medical Officer to look out for any man who had wounds across his fingers because he might be a culprit. Of course, the rumour quickly spread far and wide and as a consequence the girls were never troubled in that way!

Identification with village people

It is interesting that Miss Hornby always liked to spend Christmas out amongst people in the villages of Kigezi. In 1924 she wrote on Christmas Day, *"I am on itineration in Bufumbira and have spent a Christmas Day after my own heart. One of my girls . . . who married the teacher lives here and if we had not come (that is my teacher Esiza and one of the other girls, Eva), she would have been the only woman in Church this Christmas Day. As it was we four women and men teachers, 8 in all, met early just for prayer, and there was an atmosphere of peace and fellowship. At 9 a.m. some 300 small boys, I believe, and a few girls came, and we had a short service. Then for an hour I talked to them in groups, and we had pictures. At 11 a.m. many followed me back to camp, and sat looking on while the teachers came and stayed till nearly 1 o'clock. Then I fed with my girls, and went visiting till night closed down."*

Miss Hornby was a real "pioneer missionary", versatile and determined. She lived in the spirit of William Carey's great sermon on Isaiah 54 vs. 2-3 which he preached at a ministers' meeting in England, 31st May 1792: *"Expect great things from God; attempt great things for God."* These words were a driving force for many missionary endeavours started in the Victorian era, and here she was following them in the 1920s in Kigezi. She had strict principles, but a soft heart and was always drawn to the poor and needy, epitomising venturesome love. She loved children and young people, constantly encouraging them and building them up. She made strong relationships both with the teachers in her School and with the girls.

The only vernacular Bibles they had at that time were in Luganda and Runyoro-Rutooro, from areas many miles away from Kigezi, but the links between Bantu languages enabled the Bakiga to understand them to some extent although not exactly their "heart language". The Runyankore-Rukiga Bible was translated by Dr Algie Stanley Smith and his team, and published in 1964. The presence of Baganda, Batooro and Banyoro teachers and Hospital workers, recruited by the two Doctors, meant that several different languages and dialects were in use. Miss Hornby had learned Luganda during her seven years based in or near Kampala, then she picked up Runyoro-Rutooro from the Bibles she used in the churches, and she learned Rukiga from the girls in the School. It is small wonder that the everyday speech she used was mixed-up and affectionately known as "Ruhornbi"! She had a good sense of humour and must have had many a laugh over misunderstandings in language.

Walking over the hills

As she felt called to outreach work to visit and stimulate village churches in the District, Miss Hornby went on "trek" frequently at weekends, leaving the School to take care of itself. Dr Stanley Smith wrote, "*It is impossible to exaggerate the importance of this work. These village churches, which number some 90 or more in the whole District, I could not possibly visit more than once or perhaps twice a year, and the teachers are for the most part far too young and untaught to be left unsupervised. So you can see what a help it is to these babes in Christ and their readers . . . when Miss Hornby goes out all over the District, shepherding these 'other' sheep.*"(Letter, early 1924)

In July 1924, Miss Hornby returned from her first itineration in Kinkiizi and Rujumbura, "*I enjoyed it very much; it certainly was a busy time, I visited some 50 churches or reading huts because that is what they are, just grass huts; sometimes there were 50 or more men and boys, and one or two girls or women in one place . . . If only a few women and girls can be won they will bring others, for indeed they can do it far better than I can, they understand each other . . . One thing was made clear, that if we do not win these women and girls before civilisation gets them, we will lose them.*"

The work was often discouraging. A previous letter says, "*There is no mass movement here among women and girls; it is a case of one by one. Hear this, and it will show you how things are. Talking to a man, and a nice man too, I asked him why not a woman or girl from his 'fence'*[14] *ever came to church or to read. Answering by a question, as a native often does, he said: 'Would you teach a cow or send a cow to church?'*" As she went around, a few girls were presented to her for her School and they became her

---

[14] "Fence" would mean a homestead surrounded by a tall, thick, protective hedge with only a narrow entrance which could be closed.

"family". Little Agenesi was an example. *"She came to me when I was on an itineration, a wee mite, very dirty, in a wee goat skin and a water pot! 'I have come' says she 'to be your child.' Of course that could not be, so I went and found her people. What a home! The father, an invalid, was sitting outside a dirty grass hut with several women and children sprawling about. I felt I must try and get her, so I boldly asked and he absolutely refused. So after much talking I came away sad. However three weeks later the child came here with a porter, and a note written by someone who could write, saying that she was to stay for three months. After three months I sent her back but she returned after two weeks and now she is my child."* (Early 1924)

Relationships and everyday life

The missionary community included little children, Mary and Joy Sharp and Nora and Eva Stanley-Smith. They all knew Miss Hornby as a family friend from their earliest years. Mary Sharp was born in March 1924 when her parents were on leave in England. She writes, *"I knew her from my babyhood at Rugarama (Kabale). She was a very much loved member of the Christian community. Like other women from Europe at that time, she wore a long dress usually with long sleeves. In the sun she wore a hat with a shady brim to protect from heat, sunburn, headaches, sunstroke or overheating from glare. She was living with and caring for all aspects of the girls' needs at Kigezi Girls' School. Each girl was committed to her care and love and teaching as if her child by relatives most of whom she had personally visited. They came from far and wide in the whole of Kigezi and also from Ruanda. Miss Hornby's School was the HOME of these girls in all ways and she became their 'Mother'".*

Mary Sharp recalls visiting and sometimes staying at Miss Hornby's house, *"I remember several times there were leopards just outside during the night. Once when she was outside her front door with her dog, a leopard took the dog from right beside her; and another time a leopard came very close to her bed by an open window on the verandah. Mostly she ate local foods, peas, beans, potatoes. She gave most of what she could to needy people so sometimes she ate very little herself. Milk was from local cows. It needed boiling. The cream was kept to make butter. If they had any bread, it was baked at the homes of the Europeans. All flour had to be ordered from Kampala. Supplies for everyone had then to be pushed on a cart with big wheels. It took three months for an 'order' to be sent and returned! At least once, flour arrived smelling of paraffin which spilt on route! Roads were not good and journeys lengthy."* (Answering a Questionnaire, May 2002)

Leave in England 1925 and the work continued

Early in 1925 Miss Hornby began to prepare to go home to England on leave. She left in March and arrived in London on June 8th, travelling by land and sea. She was very sad to leave her girls behind with no one to keep the School running, and so, fearing that they would run away, she decided to take them to Gayaza High School for safe keeping. According to Jean Hurford and Margaret Oliver who heard the story from her own lips, "*She walked them all to Gayaza in Kampala. It took several days, sleeping at homes of chiefs en route. When they reached Masaka they were able to get a lorry. When she returned, she collected them from Gayaza and took them back to Kabale. She remembered all their names and families.*" (Questionnaires 2002/August 2010).

In England she stayed at her parents' home in Twickenham. She wrote some of her impressions in a short letter to the Ruanda Mission supporters, "*One thing which strikes me now that I am really back is the wonderful goodness of the many who help those who are working abroad. Another thing is the amount that is spent by this very much alive people on pleasure; and another is how some really sincere Christian people fear to frighten our young people with the word 'Missionary'.*" She had a long list of "wants" and she stressed that she would do all she could to see that any gifts would be used aright. Accountability and transparency were as important then as they are in the 21st Century. She closed the letter saying, "*I hope to return in December. I get such sad letters from the girls who are counting the "Moons" until I return. We need money to build a school, but I will not say more because so many are doing so much to help build the Church.*" (July 8th, 1925) The last sentence refers to the work of Rev. Jack Warren who arrived on his motorbike as a new missionary in time for Christmas 1924 and had raised much of the funding to build St Peter's Church. He was greatly involved in the building work which was supervised by Dr Len Sharp. By June 1926 the walls were finished and the frame of the roof in place. His other work was in teaching boys at Kigezi High School. He was a great enthusiast and is warmly remembered.

Back to beloved Kigezi

Miss Hornby enjoyed her leave and wrote from the ship S.S. Mulbera at Marseilles on New Year's Day 1926, impressed by the hospitality received, "*I can never express my thanks, but as I went here and there all over*

England it was always the same, in fact I got 'spoilt'." Her first task would be to go to Gayaza to collect her girls and then go round Kigezi District getting new ones. She was now attached to the Girls' Friendly Society as their "own missionary" as explained in Chapter Three. As soon as she arrived in Kabale, she organised a safari with Eseza her Head Teacher and set off, experiencing hospitality from local people on the way. *"Again – I am sorry to confess that it is nearly always my madness that does it – I had arranged to visit two reading huts between camps, and I told the readers at the third to come over a huge hill and meet me. Somehow or other the messenger never got out, but as I wanted to see the readers of Kiogi I just went to them. It was a march! Right over a huge hill and back again! Instead of getting into camp at eleven, at one I was still on the road that passed the home of Agenesi, who is known to many of you. You will understand that I wanted to see her, but my pluck began to give out. She settled the matter, however, by rushing out to meet me and taking me to her home. Food was just being served and I was invited to eat. I did not need a second invitation. We sat on the floor, washed our hands, and ate peas, beans and potatoes. I had left camp at 5.45 a.m. and I did not arrive back until 3 p.m., but I was quite fit – thanks to Agenesi's people."*

Visitors from England came to Kabale in 1926 and gave this report on the Girls' School: *"Miss Hornby single-handed trains and teaches thirty-three boarders, besides day scholars, aged from 5 to 18. Seven of the girls are prospective brides, whose fiancés, Christian men, have brought them from heathen homes to be taught for one year before being married. It is most interesting to see the differences in the faces of those who have been in the School some time. Cleanliness and hope take the place of dirt and despair. It is all important that Christian men should be able to find Christian wives. The Boys' Boarding School, under the Rev. J.E.L. Warren, is doing a similar work among the boys."* (D. & A. Stather Hunt, Ruanda Notes, 1927)

The Story of the Warren Family

On January 1st, 1927, a huge crowd of about 2,000 people gathered at St Peter's Church for the wedding of Rev. Jack Warren to Dr Kathleen Ardell. It was the first service to be held in the great new Church and it was beautifully decorated by Mrs Guillebaud, assisted by many others, using arum lilies and fronds of papyrus. Miss Hornby was most likely in the congregation and she became a good friend of the newly weds. Indeed, she was pleased to use her skills as a midwife. It is recorded in the old Visitors' Book of Jack and Kathleen Warren that she stayed in their home from November 23rd, when baby Sheelagh was born, until December 3rd. The Warren family lived in a large mud and wattle house with a thatched roof. It was improved over the years and "The Warren" later became a boarding house of Kabale Preparatory School. They had a car and he drove it round and round the Hill in his delight. Sadly, Jack had TB which he contracted in the First World War through being gassed and he had to go home in June 1928, when Sheelagh, future Headmistress of Gayaza High School, was 6 months old. He died in Walmer in England in January 1929 when she was 14 months old. Her mother who was a medical doctor, took her to Kenya at the end of 1933. Then, in January 1935, she was asked to go back to Ngora where she had worked before her marriage. Sheelagh was sent to school in England and was there until 1957 when she went with C.M.S. to Gayaza High School.[15]

WEDDING OF REV. JACK WARREN TO DR KATHLEEN ARDELL, JAN. 1ST 1927. [PHOTO BY DR LEN SHARP 1923, FROM THE ARCHIVES, BISHOP BARHAM UNIVERSITY COLLEGE]

[15] Details supplied by Sheelagh Warren, former Headmistress of Gayaza High School, to complete the story.

Plenty of Variety in Life (1927)

Miss Hornby went on with her weekend treks and little details in her letters to the G.F.S. show how simply she lived. *"The Branch which gave me the chant book and wee cup is always in my memory . . . The book I use daily when on the station and the cup daily when off. It is much easier to get water from a stream with a cup than with one's hand, and it fits into my pocket finely."* (Jan. 6th 1927) That year was the Golden Jubilee of the Church of Uganda with big celebrations in Kampala. Her letters in June and July include comments on the School, *"I sometimes think we've the very naughtiest school in the world. I read of India, all the girls are good; of South Africa, Japan etc. and always all the girls are good. Now listen . . ."* She describes some lively behaviour, such as one girl taking a teacher's words the wrong way and a class drawing spectacles on their faces in chalk. She continues, *"They are absolutely fearless, at least Eseza says that they do not fear enough, but they take punishment like sportsmen. We now number 57. I do not have an inch of room left."* June was the time of the Jubilee and Miss Hornby held the fort in Kabale when others went away. *"June 29th. I've taken over a big job from June 18th to July 5th. I'm running the hospital and all the people have gone to Kampala for the Jubilee. We broke up on the 20th, so I have no school to think about and so far all has gone well and I am learning quite a lot. No one has died therefore I have killed no one. I hope to get away on trek about July 7th, when I have handed over."*

By October, the school had 62 girls and the dormitory thatched roof slipped causing them to shift to the schoolroom, using the dilapidated building for lessons until the materials could be brought together for a new roof. She gave out prizes in each class so that girls could earn books, bags, pencils, a cloth or a dress from the parcels received. *"Reading, Writing, Handicrafts, three best cooks, one best digger, one best dormitory girl. There is also a prize for conduct and two for Sunday school, so with 62 girls about 46 prizes are given."* She longed for someone to help her in the multifarious tasks, even playing games with the girls. *"I've to make all the dresses. I am trying to teach Blandina to use my sewing machine but I am very afraid. Next year if she does not get married I believe she will be able to do almost anything."* As the time for another Leave was on the horizon she felt burdened. *"I dare not leave sixty girls for long."* She longed for a "DREAM LADY" to come out from England to take over the school. Christmas was approaching, *"Did I ever tell you about the star? I had been teaching the younger ones the story of the Wise Men, and I said we did not see stars journeying like that. 'O yes, we do,' said one, 'they often fall down on their journey and I've caught them.' This I could not agree to. Three days later the child rushed into my room (no knock). 'Oh, I've caught one and brought it to you. Now you'll believe.' It was a fire-fly."*

Developments in 1928

In the same edition of *Ruanda Notes*, the name of a new recruit was announced: *"A helper, the "Dream Lady" of the above letter has been found. Miss Margaret Forbes hopes to be ready to sail next May to 'lend a hand'."* Miss Hornby's delight overflowed, but meanwhile she had to bear the loss of her other helper, *"Good trustworthy Blandina leaves me to be married in April. She is a Mukiga, and her people drove her away in 1923, and she has been my child ever since. Anything I asked her to do I knew would be done faithfully. Last May the relations came to see me and ask if Blandina might go back to them in the holidays. But I said: "You drove her away, and four years ago in my presence you said to her 'Choose, stay here and leave the Christians or go with them and never return. We will have no Christians in our fence.' Now they cannot make enough of her. The man she wants to marry is a teacher."* (Jan. 13th 1928) The date for her wedding was fixed for July 7th, but it was put off because the cows needed for the dowry were in quarantine. *"For my own sake I am glad, but I must go and have a talk with her people . . . "* (June 3rd 1928) The wedding was put off again, and Blandina returned to Kabale Girls' School.

The year went on with joys and sorrows. *"We have to say 'The Lord gave and the Lord has taken away' but I have to swallow very hard before I can say 'Blessed be the name of the Lord', for on June 4th one of our little ones went to Jesus. She was one of our youngest and brightest . . . "* (July 1st 1928) In the same letter she describes an exciting adventure on one of her treks. *"We had a long hard march right through a great bamboo forest and over a huge hill so we set off at dawn. Having climbed the hill and dropped into the plain we found several men sitting there who said: 'We can't go on as there is a herd of elephant on the road.' I only laughed and walked on and they joined us. All was well for half an hour when in front of us we saw a great elephant slowly moving through the forest . . . we soon saw there were others in the forest. The wind was blowing from us to them and the elephant turned and looked as if he were coming towards us. This was too much for the porters and they dropped their loads and ran. My headman and the girls begged me to go back but I would not give in. The elephant walked up and down for a little, talking to those in the forest, and I said 'Go and fetch the porters back and I will wait until you have all passed.' When they had all got past the elephant lifted up his trunk and went after the herd. The porters went on at a great pace and I followed on my bicycle . . ."* The herd went ahead, then turned into the forest and the intrepid missionary and her party escaped unscathed! It may have been the occasion of the story when she forgot to say a prayer of thanksgiving and was reminded by her girls, "Miss Hornby, we prayed for protection as we set off, don't you think we should thank the Lord Jesus now?" She humbly obeyed, perhaps realising how great a risk she had taken by leading her girls and the rest of the party into such danger.

ELEPHANTS IN KIGEZI.
*[PHOTO ROGER F.L.
WILKINS]*

The latter half of 1928 was a hard time in the school. Miss Hornby wrote in her December letter about the girls' misbehaviour, talking and playing in the dormitory after the "Silence" bell, then being generally uncooperative during daily Prayers which she was leading. Miss Hornby was angry, refused to go on and dismissed the school to reading classes. Soon after, they had thieves in their food store at night who stole peas, beans and a box of ground millet. She wrote, *"Unfortunately, Dr Sharp was on safari, but his head man went all round. But all peas and beans look alike also ground millet, so it was our loss; but it pulled us together again and the family were sorry. So you see none of us are just what we ought to be. We have big patches of bad in us and I only hope that Miss Forbes will be able to help us to reduce on the bad patches."* There is a lot of realism and honesty in her relationships with others. She may have had difficulty with discipline because she was not a trained teacher but by building a "family" which included all the girls from any background she won their loyalty which continued throughout their lives and extended to "grandchildren"; she had seven by 1928. The story of the girls of the early years could be followed up and would reveal the extent of her godly influence far and wide.

A significant safari

Sometime in 1929 she went on a trek to Rujumbura and visited Kyamakanda. A ten-year old herd-boy named Kivengere, grandson of the great Chief of the Bahororo named Makobore, with his friend Bugaari hid in the long grass, eager to see her. They had been warned by their parents to be very careful that day because a "pink lady" was approaching. They feared she might eat them. They watched intently and observed her extraordinary headgear (a pith helmet), her pale colour and her piercing blue eyes as she was carried past in a kind of sedan chair,[16] with porters bearing her luggage behind. At the village, she received a cautious welcome from the chiefs. She handed out sweets and began to explain her mission seeking girls to take to her school in Kabale. This may have been the visit when a bright little girl named Mera (or Merabu) Nyinenzangi was enrolled. She was from a high-born family among the Bahororo. Both Kivengere and Mera will enter the story of Miss Hornby's life several times as the years go by.

Preparations for Leave

Miss Hornby as a C.M.S. missionary had overseas leave every five years. The next one was due from December 1st 1929. She welcomed Miss Margaret Forbes' arrival to take over during her absence,[17] and another helper, Miss King, is also mentioned. Miss Forbes wrote in her first letter (May 1929) *"Just now the school is very full, but I expect some of the older girls will soon be leaving to be married. They are an awfully jolly crowd and chatter like magpies . . . the school girls here are perfectly natural, in fact they are one big family. The other Sunday night one of the matrons came to Miss Hornby with the news that Cucu (one of the most mischievous children) was lost. She was last seen at supper, and then had vanished into thin air. It was nearly dark and everyone was out hunting for her. At last Miss Hornby said it was impossible for*

---

[16] Sedan chair: used in England in 17th and 18th Century, a chair for one person carried by two chairmen with poles. (Concise Oxford Dictionary)

[17] Miss Forbes would have had a bi-lingual language helper to translate what she was saying into Rukiga, the language of the Bakiga of Kigezi district. Teaching was done in the vernacular language until the 1940s, but the girls would have learned English as a subject.

a child to disappear like that, and that she must be somewhere in the buildings, and then a muffled chuckle was heard. Turning round she discovered Cucu huddled up in a box used for storing peas, thoroughly enjoying the joke."

The year went on and the time for farewells came. Miss Hornby wrote in the Christmas holiday, *"We lifted up our voices together and wept, and now it is over. I have tried to break my connection with them slowly . . . and yet it was a nasty jar when I left. Some of those bairns I have known for years, Agenesi, Keziya, Blandina and others since 1923 and they have grown up with me."* She went on a last trek in January 1930 and visited an old girl named Tafasi. *"Her second baby arrived only a few hours before I did (our 21st grandchild) a dear little girl; I bathed her and she almost spoke she was so wide awake . . . It does not seem five years since I took Tafasi to Mbarara on my way home last time; a child then and now the mother of two babies. Danieri is only twenty months old."* She then travelled to Kampala and from there to Tanganyika for a holiday before boarding the S.S. Madura at Dar es Salaam. *"I am coming with a wonderful scheme in my mind so tell everyone that I shall want all their splendid help as in time past."* The Editor of *Ruanda Notes* added that she arrived safely looking very well.

Looking Ahead

A turning point in the history of God's work in Kigezi had been reached. Dr Algie Stanley Smith wrote with foresight in mid 1929: *"The work in Kigezi is passing through a time of testing through adverse circumstances; and a good deal of what was unworthy and not spiritual has come to light, and many have fallen away. One realises more than ever the utter worthlessness of any work which is not the work of the Holy Spirit; and you can do no greater work for us than to pray Him to come down upon us and our people as at Pentecost. But the testing time is proving the reality of those who are true; and when they are tried, 'they shall come forth as gold'."* There was a wave of prayer for several years. In his own time, God answered.

Canon Peter Rwabyoma sums up the situation, *"In a nutshell, Christianity had arrived. Africans embraced it in large numbers – but sadly there was no evident spiritual transformation. As the saying goes, 'History repeats itself, simply because we don't listen the first time.' The situation was spiritually pathetic; and that's when in God's timing His Spirit moved amongst our desperate semi-Christian believers. This movement of the Holy Spirit was, and still is known as 'The East African Revival Movement'. Constance Hornby was caught up in it – and what was her candid experience during that epoch in the Christian history of Christianity among the Bakiga of Kigezi?"* (Paper, 2009)

Chapter Five
1930 – 1935
CARRY ON, MISS HORNBY!

A memorable Rally

Miss Hornby arrived in England in April and made her base at her parents' home in Twickenham, a pleasant suburb of London on the north bank of the River Thames. Her goal was to visit as many Branches of the Girls' Friendly Society as possible, sharing news of the School at Kabale and the Old Girls. Within the year she travelled tirelessly and made over 80 visits. By the end, 67 Branches were sending financial support for her work to the G.F.S. Uganda Fund. They paid to the C.M.S. enough to cover her travel and allowances for the coming year. The girls who belonged to G.F.S. diligently collected or made the many Magyar dresses,[1] knickers, dolls and other things she mentioned, sending parcels out to Uganda. Miss Hornby was an inspiring speaker with many stories to tell and she gained strength from the love and encouragement of the members. She asked for their constant prayers and pledged to do all she could as their Own Missionary. It was a close relationship. *"Some of us who were in Manchester on October 25th, 1930, remember your President's wonderful command. I can hear those papers now as they were waved and the sound of many, many voices as one which said "Carry on!" I'm here to carry on for you if all is well for four more years, and I know you'll all "carry on" away in England. Oh! Your people here are so young and with so little to help them in their lives, we just rely on you. I, that I may not be impatient, and they, that they may get hold of the Greatest thing of all, and 'put up' with me."* (Kabale, April 1931)

A lively sense of humour

Miss Hornby was not always serious and her sense of humour was ever active. In London in the 1930s there were many branches of a

---

[1] According to the Concise Oxford Dictionary, a dress with the sleeves cut in one piece with the main part of the garment. (Magyar, pronounced 'modyar', means 'Hungarian', and the dresses typically resemble Hungarian native costume.)

popular Restaurant, Lyons Corner House, and a little joke arose. It was reported in *Ruanda Notes* December 1930: *"Miss Hornby has been doing far too much while on furlough. A week or two ago a lady came up to her after a meeting and asked, 'Do you have lions in Africa?' 'Lyons?' said Miss Hornby in a puzzled voice, 'Oh no, our station is nearly 300 miles beyond the end of the railway and the only shops we have are a few little Indian stores!'"* Another version of this story ends, *"Lyons? Oh no, we bake our own bread."* Before she left, a studio photograph was taken and it is the only one to appear in the Mission magazine for many years. She is neatly dressed. Her kindly, open face radiates energy and compassion. At age 46 she looks younger than her years, an attractive, efficient-looking person.

CONSTANCE HORNBY,
1931. [*RUANDA NOTES,
C.M.S. ARCHIVES*]

The system of Education in Uganda

This is a suitable juncture to include some basic information about Educational Policy in Uganda so that we can understand the context to which Miss Hornby returned after her leave. The first schools were all founded by missionaries and the Government contributed grants to them. In 1924 the Phelps-Stokes Commission visited Uganda, a group of educationalists including the famous Dr Aggrey from the Gold Coast. Their purpose was to analyse the educational progress in each country of Africa and to advise the Governments on future policy. Their 400 page Report was not fulsome in praise of the work done in Uganda, *"Only a good beginning has been made"*, they said. They urged the Government to set up a Department of Education under a Director and to increase its financial involvement from the meagre 2% of its annual expenditure allowed at the time. They insisted that education should be tailored to the needs of the community and the enhancement of African culture. They stressed the importance of Agricultural training, Hygiene and Health. They listed five Aims of Education:

The Aims of Education according to the Phelps-Stokes Commission 1924

1. The development of character on the foundation of Religion
2. The improvement of health
3. The acquisition of agricultural and industrial skill
4. The improvement of family life
5. "Sound and healthful recreations" which include music.

The first Director of Education was Mr Hussey. He tried to implement these ideals and met opposition both from African opinion which saw education as the way of escape from toil on the land, and from the European teachers who wanted to share the best of their own culture and heritage and who tended towards a more academic approach. They developed boarding schools upon the pattern of the English Public Schools including the Prefect system and games such as Cricket, Football, Tennis and, for girls, Netball. Diagrammatically, a pyramid of schools had been developed in the 1920s, at its apex the Government College (for boys only) at Makerere, a few Intermediate schools (also for boys) and below them the Normal Schools which made provision for Teacher Training. Part of Gayaza High School at that time was known as a "Normal School". At the base of the pyramid were the many Elementary Schools, of which Miss Hornby's would be one when recognised by the Government. Below that level were the "bush schools" set up by the missionaries and Church leaders to teach reading in the simple church buildings put up by local communities. Although Miss Hornby herself was not a trained teacher, she would certainly have agreed with the Aims shown above. She wrote in 1928 to the Girls' Friendly Society, *"Our life is a very busy one; from 5.30 a.m. to 7 p.m. all booked up. You see we dig and grow our own food, fetch our own water and cook, as well as school, but I believe they are really happy . . . All are keen on G.F.S. They know what it stands for, and we use the text on the Calendar at evening prayers . . . We do the Scripture Competition in school. If as a whole, we could compete, you folk in England would not have a look in; we would be first always! I love to think of G.F.S. prayers going up for these girls."* She made character training a priority, taught the girls personal hygiene and prepared many of them to be Christian wives and mothers.

The Report of the Department of Education 1928 says of girls' schools, *"They want them to assimilate by association with European women the manners and habits of wives and mothers in a civilized state."* Miss Hornby lived with her girls and taught them all that she considered good, but her main aim was not "civilisation" but to lead them to faith in Jesus Christ and to live under his sway. As seen in Chapter Four, she believed in identification with her pupils leading to relationships within which the message of the Gospel would be communicated.

It was clear both to the Government and to the leaders in the Church that educated men needed educated wives, otherwise there would be a disaster in society. Most ordinary people thought that only their sons should go to school and their daughters should stay at home to grow food. However, some perceived that Ugandan girls for their own sake deserved to be educated as much as their brothers. There were few careers open for girls at that time, although nursing and teaching were opening up. It was a great step forward when two of her girls, Agenesi and Keziya, went to Gayaza to study for the Teacher's Certificate in 1930. Miss Hornby was one of a long line of educational pioneers in world history who fought for education for women and girls. In Uganda, the development of girls' education followed the same pattern as the boys' but at a slower pace. It took until 1937 for the first girl to enter Secondary School and until 1945 for one to pass the Senior Secondary Leaving Examination and enter Makerere College. But that is jumping ahead of our story.

Return to Kigezi 1931

During Miss Hornby's leave, the building of the Kenya and Uganda Railway was going ahead. In 1928 it reached the River Nile near Jinja and a great Bridge was constructed in 1930, using materials brought from England, and the railway line was extended to Kampala. The Bridge was designed to carry the road as well as the railway. It was opened by the Governor on January 14th 1931. Meantime, Miss Hornby was at sea. She reached Mombasa then, continuing in her own words, *"We travel by train for three days. You try to sleep in spite of the noise and the heat. You get very very dirty, but you keep moving. The engine 'eats' wood, and at night the sparks from the funnel are like golden rain . . . Yesterday I went over the Bridge . . . It has just been finished and was opened last month. We went across it very very slowly. It is made of iron and has only a single line, but you get a magnificent view of the Ripon Falls, which rush along at one side."* (February 28th 1931) She arrived in Kampala and made a point of going to Gayaza to see Agenesi and Keziya. *"They were very pleased to see me, but they could not speak a single word, and they cried badly when I left. However, I've promised that they shall come to Kabale for their first holidays, and they'll soon settle down again."* When she reached Kabale, she had a great welcome back to the School which had fared well under Miss Forbes and she soon settled down to work.

Relationships: the key to effective mission work

Through her training and experience with the Church Missionary Society, Miss Hornby knew very well that fruitful Christian service depended upon good relationships. She returned from her leave, during which she had lived at home with her parents but had mingled with hundreds of other people and had travelled far and wide, and found herself in a close-knit community of missionaries and Africans. She happened to be about six years older than both Dr Sharp and Dr Stanley Smith, who were born in 1890, but she was always loyal to their leadership. Nevertheless, she was regarded as a Senior Missionary, a somewhat revered position in the eyes of younger members of the Mission. We have seen that she tended to have strongly-held views. She may not have been the easiest person to have on the Mission Station.

Dr Joe Church in his memoirs tells of two incidents in 1928 both concerning a leopard. He was young, enthusiastic and impressionable on arrival at Kabale. He followed Dr Sharp around, learning all he could.

"Big game hunting was on the time-table as well as language study, hospital outreach and visits to village churches. I brushed aside one or two criticisms – that hunting was too dangerous and was it really necessary? I loved every minute of it especially when I was with someone whom I looked up to immensely as a man of God like Leonard Sharp. But God brought a challenge to me through the Irish[2] forthrightness of Constance Hornby, a senior missionary, who had leanings towards 'anti-vivisection' and was against hunting of any kind". He built a trap for a troublesome leopard near the mission station incorporating a live goat as a lure, and a gun to shoot it first. *"It was the night of fear for the small goat that Miss Hornby tried to get me to see. In the argument that followed she overstated her case by saying, 'I don't mind what happens to you but it is bringing suffering to the animals . . .' This remark stuck in my mind and comes into the story later when I was carried into Kabale having been badly mauled by a leopard."*

Dr Church was posted to Gahini Hospital in Ruanda. One Sunday in October 1928 he was called out to rescue frightened villagers from attack by a big, old leopard. He took Kosiya Shalita (later to become Bishop of Ankole) on the back of his motorbike and went in pursuit. They did kill the wild animal but it jumped on top of Dr Joe in its wounded state and mauled him. He had to be taken to Kabale Hospital for an operation and whilst convalescing had time to think and pray about many things. *"One of them was my lack of oneness with Constance Hornby. I wrote a note to her and asked her to forgive me for unwillingness to take her challenge about hunting and that her remark, that she didn't mind what happened to me, had kept coming back to my mind and especially now that I had almost met my end! Round she came and sat by my bed, and all was rolled away by the love of God, and then we could laugh again. I think that I began to get better quicker too. From that day God helped us to be one."*[3]

Rev. Lawrence Barham's first impressions

Another young missionary at Kabale, Rev. Lawrence Barham, also knew Miss Hornby. In a letter to the Mission dated 4th November 1929 he says, *"I am now installed in the jolly little two-roomed house Miss Hornby has built here at our centre in Rujumbura. It is well-built (of course: Miss*

---

2   In our researches, we found no information about Irish descent of the Hornby family. They came from the North of England where people are known for plain speaking.

3   Church, *Quest of the Highest* p. 30 and 44.

Hornby built it!) and very cosy." He was obviously an admirer of her practical skills and like many others in years to come grateful for the strongly constructed small houses, just a bedroom and a sitting room

MISS HORNBY'S HOUSE AT SESEME, KISORO IN 1972 (WITH THE AUTHOR, THEN TEACHING AT KIGEZI HIGH SCHOOL)

VIEW FROM MISS HORNBY'S HOUSE TOWARDS THE VOLCANOES, MUHAVURA AND MGAHINGA, 1972. *[PHOTO: E. TRAILL]*

with outside kitchen, toilet and shelter for washing, which she caused to be built at several Church centres in Kigezi. He also tells of a "Week of Prayer" towards the end of 1929 held in four centres including Kabale before Miss Hornby went away on leave. *"Addresses were given each day, but chiefly we spent the time in prayer, and there seemed a real desire for something better."* Undoubtedly, she would have taken a full part in this and shared with the team in its spiritual yearnings. Dr Sharp, whom she respected very much, wrote in 1931 when there was a delay in obtaining Government permission to extend the work to new centres, *"We here are feeling increasingly the need of new Power from on high – a greater devotion to Christ – more prayer revival, and it may well be that this time of waiting over the sites is intended in God's purpose to bring us to our knees more than ever in repentance, confession and supplication, so that when advance is made it may be in the Power of God and not in the wisdom and energy of man. Daniel's prayer was needed before Ezra and Nehemiah could build Jerusalem. 'Continuing daily with one accord in prayer' by the apostles was necessary to the first spread of the Gospel . . ."*

Identification with the people

Although she was one in heart and spirit with her fellow missionaries, Miss Hornby lived in her own house and spent most of her time with her girls and staff at the School, and with her team on long treks through the villages on foot. As we have seen, she even preferred to spend Christmas at one of the village churches rather than joining in the European family fun at the mission station. She was always very interested in the Medical side of the work and would have rejoiced at the opening of the Leprosarium on Bwama Island, Lake Bunyonyi, in 1930, with two dedicated nurses, Miss May Langley and Miss Horton. She was ever ready to help in time of need, as seen in the previous chapter when she willingly took charge of the Hospital so that other missionaries could go to Kampala for the Jubilee celebrations of the Church of Uganda in 1927. For the month of January 1933 she replaced Miss Sadler, Matron of the Hospital, so that she could go to Bwama Island to cover Miss Langley's holiday.

Miss Hornby made it her aim to identify with the people and to live as closely as possible as they did in order to share Jesus Christ with them. How strong were her relationships with her African colleagues? In her letters, she calls them by their Christian names, Eseza, Dolosi, Blandina, Agenesi and Keziya and others, whereas she never uses

Christian names for other missionaries, always Miss Forbes, Dr Sharp and so on. We may wonder if there was a hidden, unconscious paternalism in her attitude. Unquestionably, she loved her staff and girls deeply. She was expert in the art of delegation, for ever building people up and giving them responsibilities and leaving them to carry on. That was how she freed herself from the ties of the School in order to go out to the villages to reach more and more women and girls with the Gospel, teaching them to read and master the basic truths so that they could be baptised and confirmed as members of the Church. In a letter dated January 15th, 1932 she writes from Seseme in Bufumbira, *"We are trying to build up our native Church and using the lava stone. It makes a good strong wall. The next thing is to work up the readers and get our teachers to understand what it is to be a teacher. We are getting about 40-50 daily readers at Seseme now. The two girl teachers have done just splendidly. They are really better to do the work than we are if only we will stand by to back them up. I have always found it quite possible to work under a native leader. All the time I was at Kabale Girls' School the work was really being done by Eseza and Dolosi. Without those two the work among the women and girls of Kigezi could never have been done. Again, here, these two girls have simply made it. I just stand by and do odd jobs."*

The fruit of good teaching

Enidi Kagobe, a Mututsi girl, was one of the two young teachers at Seseme. Miss Forbes mentioned her in a letter dated November 14th, 1930: *"Quite a number of girls have left us to be married, and are now happily settled in their own homes. I wish you could see these Christian homes: the contrast between them and the ordinary kraals is extraordinary. They are clean and tidy and often have bright pictures on the wall, but above and beyond that, one feels that Christ is indeed the Head of the home. At Christmas one of our very faithful teachers, Freda, is being married to a man who works near here. Enidi may be leaving too, so there will have to be a re-arrangement of classes all round. Both these teachers have done very good work, and have been getting really dependable, so their going will leave a big gap. On the other hand it will give some of the older girls a chance to take their turn in responsible positions in the school."*

We may be surprised by the way the school was run and the teachers were trained. Miss Forbes continued, *"I always devote Monday morning to the teachers, but when they only know very little more than their pupils, this time is spent in preparing the lessons for the coming week. A rather 'hand to mouth' system of teacher training!"*

It seems that Enidi and her colleague had an uphill task as teachers. Miss Hornby wrote in 1932, *"They have between twenty-four and thirty-four, according to the work in the fields. It is always a problem for the women and girls, as the fields have to be looked after, for their food is their income really, so at certain times the girls are at work from sun up to sun set."* She continued, *"I am troubled about Enidi's house. The girls are doing really well and seem to cluster. She knows her girls and all about them. Yesterday there were 39 present. The teacher's hut, however, must be on an underground river, and we cannot get it dry, so it means that we, i.e. G.F.S., must shift it and hope for a nice dry place."*

However, marriage beckoned and Enidi left in March 1933. *"She will be a great loss to the school work...her people love her. I have had to send Blandina Kakazi there to carry on for three months. She is a Mukiga. Oh dear, why must our teachers get married?... And yet I am glad if they marry good men ..."* Miss Hornby faced all kinds of different challenges from day to day, but always seemed to have the grace to rise above them and to see the good which would come as a result of the changes which took place in her work.

An inspiring poem

Faraway, in South India, another lady missionary named Amy Carmichael was working amongst women and girls, rescuing some children one by one from heathen temples. In the 1930s, she wrote many books and poems, bound in a distinctive blue. Copies were circulated among the missionaries at Kabale and it is most likely that Miss Hornby read the books and shared her spirit. One of the poems says,

> *"Give me the love that leads the way,*
> The faith that nothing can dismay,
> The hope no disappointments tire,
> The passion that will burn like fire,
> Let me not sink to be a clod:
> Make me Thy fuel, Flame of God."[4]

The coming of modern technology

Miss Hornby also needed strong faith and resourcefulness during all the changes in the 1930s. Modern technology was gradually reaching

---

[4] Houghton,Frank: *Amy Carmichael of Dohnavur* p. 36.

Kigezi. On April 8th 1932 two R.A.F. seaplanes[5] circled over Lake Bunyonyi taking photographs. Dr Len Sharp described the reaction of the people, *"No aeroplanes had ever been over Kigezi before. At first they thought they were looking at great and unknown birds, but when they realized that there were people flying in the heaven, some of the Bakiga thought it must be the Lord's return. The sudden and miraculous appearing of people in the sky flying with incredible speed and great noise did seem to them at first a sign of His Coming."*

SEAPLANE ON LAKE BUNYONYI, 1932.
[PHOTO BY DR LEN SHARP, BISHOP BARHAM UNIVERSITY COLLEGE ARCHIVES]

This dramatic event passed into the folklore and songs of the Bakiga, one traditional dance being called "Enyonyi" after the first aeroplanes. Miss Hornby moved with the times and acquired a motor car (affectionately known as "my bus"), which was a great help for her long safaris to the Centres such as Kinyasaano in Rujumbura in the north, Seseme in Bufumbira, the south-west and Bukinda in Rukiga, on the road to Kampala from Kabale. In March 1933 she was the driver for Enidi's wedding in Rujumbura, leaving Kabale at 7.30 a.m. with the

---

[5] R.A.F. stands for the Royal Air Force from the United Kingdom. These aeroplanes had floats as well as wheels, so that they could land on water.

bride and Rev. Ezekiel Balaba the pastor. They had a good journey going and the wedding was splendid, but on the way back they were held up by a storm: *"For a whole hour we had to stop, then the road newly made, was loose and soft, and for twenty miles it was skid, skid, skid, and at last I could not drive any more . . . I rested half an hour, and we did a good bit of road. Then the trouble started . . . In a mile and a half we got stuck in the mud five times, and we had something like thirty men helping to dig us out and push; but the last time, which was worst of all, I slipped and broke my clutch "away in the blue". A Roman Catholic Father happened to come along. He was not able to mend my bus but got a whole crowd of his readers to push me to his place, and there I am for the night . . . "* The next day, she and her companions walked back to Kabale!

Some difficulties in her work

Miss Hornby was a principled lady. In her relationships with African women and girls she aimed not to make dependants. She explained this principle in a letter written in 1932: *"This morning three girls came to me from a far-off village and wanted to work for books. One, a confirmed girl, wanted a Bible, and the other two New Testaments . . . It is good for them to do something towards them, so I have arranged that they work for a few days, and I will pay them in books. One of our young widows with two year old twin boys slipped and broke her leg, so I am arranging for them to work in her garden. Please don't think I'm hard in this; oh, no, we want to help the folk to help themselves . . . If we teach them to beg they'll do it. But if we show them how to get money and ease the burden for them, they'll do it. They are very teachable and I dread the thought of spoiling them by always giving . . . Away in the country I make them bring a grass mat they have made. It is only worth about 2 pence, but it has cost them their time . . . I must have something to help me to know if a girl is just lazy or if she really cannot help herself. If she really and truly wants a New Testament she'll go to the swamp and get grass and make a mat."*

Starting a new school in North Kigezi

The same principle had to be put into practice when it came to schooling. Also in 1932 she went to Rujumbura to help a new teacher start a school. Merabu Nyinenzangi had performed very well at Kabale Girls' School and had been sent to Gayaza High School for six months of teacher training. Now she was to be a very young Headmistress. Miss Hornby wrote to the G.F.S. from Kinyasaano, *"We've got six slates, and a packet of needles, and a mark book, and also your teacher who is a very happy, bright girl – one of your old girls. Go on backing her up, for she has a hard pull before her. I shall not stay with her for long, and dearly as I love these folks, I know they don't want to be taught just for love of learning. Already three have said 'Give us clothes and we'll come,' and when I said, 'No, my children, we cannot,' they just said 'Well, we'll go elsewhere!' . . . If these girls come and really want to be taught, we must put up a building, but we are going to wait three months and see."* Her strategy worked. *"Merabu has in one month got 17 girls to read daily, some from 7 to 9 a.m., others from 3.30 to 5.30 p.m., and she will slowly get more. She will have to use her organising powers to keep her five classes going as some have gone ahead, and some new ones will have come, and it will be difficult for one teacher to manage . . . She herself is but a girl of 16, but a fine girl, always merry and bright."* Later in the year she sent an appeal to the G.F.S. for Magyar dresses in unbleached calico for Sunday best at Merabu's school, also for Seseme. *"Merabu has got together a truly wonderful little school all by herself. A number of girls, big and little, come daily to be taught. She has got a native handcraft class making clay cooking pots and plaited mats. Her idea is to get money to buy each girl a dress for Sundays. Well, a cooking pot only sells for five cents or ten, it is a long job. Then your letter came while I was thinking, and I talked it out with her, and we decided to help and give them dresses and the money they make must buy soap."* In May 1933, on the day after Enidi's wedding, already mentioned, Miss Hornby paid a visit to Merabu's school: *"On the ground on either side of the door were things that the girls had modelled. One was a wonderful cow . . . it was almost perfect with the ears and horns in the right places . . . the mats and the sewing were far ahead of the Kabale Boarding School, but the writing was not so good. In December there were only ten girls who were learning their letters, now they can read the first Reader. The discipline is wonderful and not one little bit of it can I claim."*

The Day School in Kabale

Great progress was also being made at the Day School in Kabale. In May 1931, Miss Muriel Barham, sister of Lawrence, arrived to work there. She had 60 women and girls coming to read, write and sew from 7-9 a.m. every morning. She commented, *"It has struck me very much how frightfully poor these people are, they have nothing of their own apart from a necklace and possibly a New Testament and sometimes a bag to put it in, and that is the beginning and ending of their possessions."* (May 20th, 1931) The following year she wrote a letter before going to Gahini to help Miss Dora Skipper for six months. The Day School had grown, *"There are now 158 on the register, and on average 100 readers every day. These people cannot be absolutely regular, as so many of them are mothers of families and there is often one child who is ill, or food which has to be got in from the fields before the heat of the day . . . God is certainly working among these people. Several women, whom I visited a few weeks ago because they were beating their daughters for coming to read, have not only allowed the girls to come, but have also come themselves and are reading every day in the school and going to Church on Sunday . . . Will you remember these people in prayer just now; it is a tremendous responsibility for the teachers, and they themselves are so young, both in years and Christian experience . . . Will you remember Lilian the Head Teacher doing a tremendous work . . . Also Doritiya, the first girl to become a teacher from the Day School; all the others are old Boarding School girls who are living near."* (Ruanda Notes, May, 1932)

One day girl's story

Dorotiya, as her name was spelt years later, married Benjamini Biteete, who worked as Headman over the church land and supervised the Hospital labour force, and they had a large family. The Biteetes were leaders in the days of the Revival and gave much service to the Church. They are a leading Christian family in the area to this day.

Dorotiya told her daughter Foibe[6] about her childhood in the hilly country of Kigezi, with swamps and rivers in the valleys. Along with other girls of her age, she taught herself to swim. As a result of attending Miss Hornby's school, she came to faith in our Lord Jesus Christ. She followed the New Testament which she bought in the school shop and felt convicted and compelled to sweep clean the house in which "Nyabingi" (the goddess of many things) supposedly lived. When her mother came back from the garden and discovered that she had swept clean that particular room she screamed in dismay, wondering what would happen to her only daughter! Dorotiya put her hand up firmly

---

[6] Source: Paper written by Mrs Foibe Rugumayo, November 2010. See Chapter Nine for further extracts.

and said, "In the name of Jesus nothing will happen to me." Indeed nothing ever happened to her. Later, following this incident her mother became a believer.

Another sad incident which Dorotiya related to Foibe concerned her step-brother Bamuturaki who did not like his sister's leanings towards the new Christianity. She and her friends would pretend they were going to work in the garden, hide their hoes on the way and attend Miss Hornby's school. Bamuturaki aware of their craftiness hid in ambush and pounced on them. He grabbed their Bibles and sadly threw them into a raging fire. Dorotiya and her friends were determined and continued to attend the school. She developed excellent handwriting under Miss Hornby's tutelage.

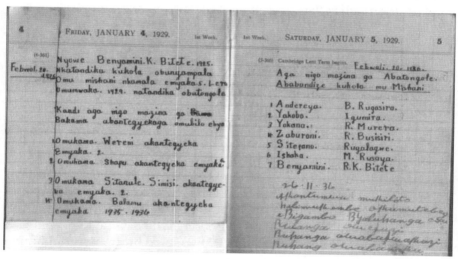

DOROTIYA BITEETE'S HANDWRITING. *[PHOTO BY PROF. E. RUGUMAYO, 2010]*

One other story comes to mind, told to us by Dorotiya herself. She became the Head Girl of the school. The incident recalls the Victorian method of Pupil Teachers. She remembered Miss Hornby instructing her how to teach some Arithmetic to the girls. "Please, Miss Hornby, I don't understand!" pleaded Dorotiya. "I didn't ask you to understand," said Miss Hornby, "Just do it!" and immediately left her for a trek to the villages. Not an example to copy, but it illustrates Miss Hornby's brisk methods on some occasions.

A thriving mission station

In April 1934 Miss Hornby gave the G.F.S. a report after ten years of work at Kabale:

"You have now-:

1. A Boarding School with 65 boarders.
2. A Girl Teachers' Training School with ten in it.
3. A Girls' Day School with from 60 to 90 in it.
4. Seven girl teachers out in village work."

She continued with details of comings and goings, marriages and building work. The dresses received had been put to good use. The girls in school obviously had a hard life, *"The girls do all the housework, digging, grinding, washing, cleaning, mending and making as well as their school work. It is a busy life."*

Indeed, everyone working on Rugarama Hill must have been very busy indeed. The Hospital was running well, Kigezi High School had 70 boys in 1933 under the leadership of P.J. Brazier and Warren Orpwood, the Girls' Boarding School[7] and the Day School were both expanding and the large Church was thronged on a Sunday. On an open slope below the Church, the Evangelists' Training School had a fine new building completed in 1934 by Rev. Lawrence Barham. The Evangelists were called "Abomushana" ("The Children of the Light") to contrast them from the superstitious pagans amongst whom they witnessed. Casual observation would have noted all this activity and imagined that all was well spiritually, but in fact there was a lot of nominalism, formality and even hypocrisy which came to be exposed during the great Revival which the Spirit of God brought to Rugarama Hill.

Everything against her

Before we enter those exciting times, consider the physical difficulties faced by Miss Hornby and others. Her letters contain little details which build into a bigger picture. She writes of a helper named Elenora who

---

[7] The amusing photograph opposite shows Lady Bourdillon entering the building with enthusiasm while Miss Hornby tries to persuade the Governor of Uganda (Sir Bernard Bourdillon, Governor from 1932–35) to come in. He seems to be more interested in his motor car!

was very close to her and was dying of consumption.[8] Several other deadly diseases were rampant and physical conditions were also hard. In the Dry Season each year, July to August, the cattle-keepers in the north of Kigezi were wont to light grass fires which polluted the air with acrid smoke. The cattle became very thin, but when the rains came they would feed with delight on the fresh green grass. She wrote in July 1931, *"I could not finish (this letter) last evening because the smoke from*

OPENING A NEW BUILDING AT THE GIRLS' SCHOOL BY THE GOVERNOR OF UGANDA. [RUANDA NOTES, C.M.S. ARCHIVES]

the grass fires nearly blinded me. This month they are always bad, but I've never before just happened to pitch my tent right in the midst." It was a bad practice and led to only very coarse, fire-resistant species of grass surviving but it would take many years to convince the Bahima not to do it. Swarms of locusts arrived from time to time and stripped the landscape of everything green. Mosquitoes troubled her at night and the dust on the dry winds made her long for a thick, still London fog like she experienced in her childhood. Shopping was very difficult when she was constantly on safari and small items which she needed (like hairpins) were hard to obtain, even salt sometimes ran out. The diet of

---

[8] Consumption was the name given to Tuberculosis which was a disease all too common and deadly in those days. The first effective drugs to combat it did not come until the 1940s.

potatoes, dried peas and beans was very monotonous. In one letter (quoted in Chapter One) she longs for a big, roasted apple! But Miss Hornby carried on despite all adversities; she was not one for giving up or complaining.

Carrying on during Times of Refreshing[9]

In response to calls from missionaries, thousands of supporters were praying for revival to come to Kabale and the other stations of the Ruanda Mission. Dr Joe Church sent out a pamphlet *Victorious Praying*, which is quoted in full in Patricia St John's beautiful book *Breath of Life* (Chapter 11). Meantime, Miss Hornby experienced many difficulties in her work. In a letter dated September 1934 she says, *"We are in sad trouble as one of our girl teachers has died. It is not her death which distresses me but the events which came before it. She, bless her, was ready to go, and I was so happy about her."* Apparently, Everini had been threatened by a man and had stood up to him, but the man hated her and sent a friend to say to her, *"'Everini, you will not see another moon.'* Two days later she was taken ill and died. We don't believe in witchcraft by charms or by words but there is a poison which witchdoctors use and her mother says, 'My girl was killed by that man.' . . . I am trying to make the poor old mother believe that it is possible for us to be poisoned, but not to be killed by small charms or crossed sticks . . . Oh! How we need to pray, 'Lighten our darkness.' I never realised what that meant in England, but now it all seems so dark."*

Indeed a battle was going on. Two of Miss Hornby's favourite hymns were *Fight the Good Fight with all thy Might* and *Onward Christian Soldiers* sung from the little hymn book named *Golden Bells*[10] which had a long section of 64 hymns entitled "Pilgrimage and Conflict". She was coming to the end of her four-year tour and was longing for her Leave, especially as the Jubilee of King George V was to be celebrated in 1935, but that was not to be. She would have loved to be in London. In March 1935 she seems rather weary, *"I just run around and yet 'old Time' rips ahead and I go to bed beaten by him night after night . . . I have had to re-roof the*

---

[9]   Words from Peter's address in Acts 3 v. 19 "Repent therefore, and turn again, that your sins may be blotted out, that times of refreshing may come from the presence of the Lord." (R.S.V.)

[10] *Golden Bells* was published by Children's Special Service Mission (Scripture Union) in 1890. The new revised edition of 1925 was commonly in use by the missionaries in Kabale, right up to the 1960s.

children's dormitory." (She describes how much she had to do herself this time in the absence of Dr Sharp, involving clambering on the half-finished papyrus roof.) *"I am not coming home until next year some time."* At the end of this letter the humanity and vulnerability of Miss Hornby comes through, *"Dark and cold, it is raining hard and I am in a tent. Much love and please forgive me, Constance Hornby."*

Other missionaries wrote reports of stirrings of the Holy Spirit amongst the Hospital staff and in the churches scattered all over the District. Lawrence Barham wrote in June 1935, *"Kabale is passing through what may be the most difficult period of its history so far; the increasing opportunities of remunerative jobs, and the greater realisation of the meaning of the Cross of Christ in the Christian life, 'By Whom the world is crucified to me and I unto the world,' are testing us, but signs are not wanting that the prayed-for revival is within sight. Pray it through!"*

The Jubilee of King George V, 1935

The Girls' School reached the end of a long 18 week term with a good health record and most enjoyable Jubilee celebrations. The District Commissioner in the name of King George gave the School a small bull for a feast, there was a march-past and a sports afternoon. In the evening Miss Hornby took 12 little girls to the Sports Ground in her car to watch the Fireworks and gathered other girls around her, explaining what would happen. The sight caused some panic in the large crowd but her girls just stood and watched. Then, Bishop Stuart and his wife came for a visit. Mrs Mary Stuart gave out the school prizes and the girls loved her. She actually made a great contribution to girls' education in Uganda. Much later on, the Women's Hall at Makerere University was named after her.

Revival Times: sharing Jesus

The story of the beginnings of the East African Revival is well documented and can be followed through in several other books. Dr Joe Church's *Quest for the Highest* is based on his own diaries and is an eye-witness account. He tells how he started teaching the great themes of the Bible, based on his Schofield Reference Bible, to the Hospital staff at Gahini in 1929. The notes developed from the sessions over the following years were made into a useful book entitled *Every Man a Bible Student*. The core message was, in his own words, *"Teaching about*

the atonement and the power of the blood of Jesus as shown in the Scriptures.[11]
At the same time he and his co-workers Yosiya Kinuka and Blasio Kigozi
wrestled in prayer and called for others to join their urgent supplications
for revival. A Convention was held at Gahini in December 1933 which
resulted in a deeper spiritual oneness in the team and a burst of
enthusiasm to take the message over the hills far and wide. News
reached Kabale and a Convention was called for evangelists and
teachers from all over Kigezi from September 22-30th 1935. It was held
in St Peter's Church which was easily large enough to hold the 400
people who attended in the day time. Probably, the nearby new
buildings of the Evangelists' Training School (now Bishop Barham
University College) were rather overcrowded at night. The daily topics
were very similar to the traditional Keswick Convention programme

A REVIVAL FELLOWSHIP MEETING ON THE TRADITIONAL PATTERN,
HELD IN ST PETER'S CATHEDRAL, 1972. *[PHOTO: E. TRAILL]*

---

[11] *Quest for the Highest,* page 84.

in England: *"Sin (Tuesday), Repentance (Wednesday), the New Birth (Thursday), 'Coming out of Egypt' Separation (Friday), the Holy Spirit and the Victorious Life (Saturday)"* There was a Gospel Service with eight testimonies on the Sunday and a Praise Meeting on the Monday before the participants went to homes, churches and bush schools with their hearts on fire and their faces shining with the love of Jesus.

A searching time

Miss Hornby knew what was happening but did not comment on it in her letters immediately. Like all the missionaries, she was keen on Bible teaching and encouraged people to buy the New Testament or the complete Bible (in Runyoro) wherever she went on her treks around the villages in the school holidays. She wrote in February 1933, *"I don't think we pray enough about the Bible, for it is now in hundreds of homes out here, and if only we prayed for it as we pray for our missionaries, it would be able to work better. Surely it – God's own Word – is the greatest missionary of all."* Regular Bible teaching took place in the schools and Baptism and Confirmation classes for which she was responsible. Ordinary Christians in Kigezi, even those with little education, from those years onwards in twice-weekly Church fellowship meetings and with their families at home have studied the Bible carefully from cover to cover and know its many stories very well. They often interpret obscure Old Testament stories in the light of the Gospel of Jesus Christ and tend to see Him on every page.

Miss Hornby was deeply involved in the spiritual battle and found that there were aspects to it which others might overlook. An example came up in mid-1934: *"There is a little girl whose mother claims she has an evil spirit inside her which is killing her. I brought her in and certainly for days she was like a mad thing, and screamed with pain and then would lie exhausted. We watched her in every way and then discovered it was tobacco. No doubt from her baby days she had been drugged with it and it was giving her an illness. We fed her up on 'obushera'[12]and in six weeks she was like an ordinary girl and wanted to do as the other girls did. We need to watch her. I*

---

[12] A nutritious drink made by the Bakiga from red sorghum which is mixed with ash, steeped in sacks in a river or swamp until it begins to sprout, then laid out in the sunshine to dry. It is then thoroughly cleaned, ground and mixed with boiling water and sometimes honey in a large earthenware pot. After a few days it is ready to drink.

would not let her go home these holidays, but one of my old married girls has offered to take her, so I hope to keep her for a whole year or more and make her use her mind." Miss Hornby was aware that the devil is a specialist in telling lies and practising counterfeit. We have seen that poison was the cause of death in Everini's case, not charms or curses. She tended to look for practical, common sense explanations and solutions to the strange goings-on associated with the Revival.

Perseverance in prayer

In the communal life of the Girls' School, sometimes spiritual blockages occurred. In mid-1934 Miss Hornby wrote, *"At 6.45 we have evening prayers for those over 11 . . . We try to get into a spirit of quiet and read a Psalm together or sing a hymn, often on our knees. Sometimes we have a Silent Time and sometimes one or two of the girls will pray. This is a great time, if it is great, but sometimes it is heavy, like a thick fog. One can feel it. Then I know that things are wrong and, sure enough, before next Prayers I hear something of this sort: 'So-and-so are hating one another' . . . 'So-and-so abused So-and-so's dead mother' . . . I tell them that 'Curses like chickens come home to roost.'"* She struggled to help people understand that becoming a Christian meant being first convicted of sin and then turning to the Saviour. One male teacher who had a sister in the Girls' School wanted her to marry a man who was not a Christian. When Miss Hornby rebuted him, he said, *"'Oh, that's all right; he is willing to become a Christian if you will let the girl go.' I could not get him to see that it is no good becoming a 'Christian' in order to get a wife – it must be from conviction of sin."*

Seeking out the lost was on Miss Hornby's heart. She enjoyed visiting her old girls with their clean homes but sometimes she had to go into filthy huts. In the same letter she wrote, *"I had to go to see a woman tonight. She was so dirty I nearly ran away. I am afraid she will die, as she has refused to be carried into hospital. Her body is thin and covered with sores and all sorts of creepy-crawlies. When she put out her hands to greet me, I nearly could not touch her but, praise be, I managed to. The teacher who was with me embraced her, her dress going right over her, and sat down beside her. I squatted down near and we tried to make the poor thing understand God's love. My! It is hard work, and somehow it gets one down. I kept remembering and remembering that woman. Tomorrow I have to go on, but your G.F.S. teacher will go and visit her regularly. She has a husband and four nice children and plenty of food, but there she is, simply filthy, dirty and ill."* Physical conditions were always against her. She continues, *"A horrid rat kept me awake the night before last and last night there was a hyena nearby. I do hope tonight will be quiet, as I want to get a good sleep before I go back to Kabale."* She had a humble approach to recent happenings. *"I dare not try to give you any account of spiritual growth, for I feel myself so much behind some of them at times, and then again at other times, these folk surprise one by doing some really un-Christlike thing. The Sermon on the Mount is pretty stiff, and that is what we are out for."*

In January 1935 she was in the far, mountainous south-west bordering the Rift Valley having enjoyed Christmas at Seseme in Bufumbira. She was ready to share the Good News wherever she could. *"A leopard killed eight goats right in front of the camp I was at yesterday, in the long grass, of course. He just killed them and, I suppose, drank the blood. That is why I hate leopards so; they kill for joy of killing, not like lions because they are hungry. Coming here today I met a little crowd of girls. They looked beautiful; they all had long strings of bright coloured beads over one shoulder and under the other arm. The cow-hide skirts were laced over one hip with strips of hide on which were threaded coloured beads. At first they were shy, but soon they told me that they had come from five miles away to get grass for making bed mats. They said they did not know who Christ was, or anything else. They said with a merry laugh: 'of course we are good.' And although it seemed awful in a lovely place and to beautiful, healthy girls to say so, I said: 'Yes, my children, but what about when you get old and die, where shall you go?' 'Do we know' they said, 'they'll just bury us.' So I tried to get it across to them that because God and Christ love us, we were not just buried like goats. They listened and said they would go to the reading-hut and hear more. Then they returned with me a little way and said 'Good bye' and soon I heard their jolly voices singing amongst the hills. These sorts of things make one realise how little we have really done."*

Another battle was to teach the girls to tell the truth on all occasions. One of them asked to go home to help her mother. She took a letter allowing her to return to the School if Miss Hornby happened to be in England at the time. *"Next I saw her working for the Government Hospital, getting a huge lot of money, and I thought that girl was one of us, but money made her lie . . . I just love every one, and to go into their dining room or dormitory is pure joy. I am making a mighty struggle to make them always speak the truth; these folk lie, and not a bit of fear or shame."* (June 1935)

Time to go on leave

The school year wore on, busy as ever. Miss Hornby was tired and did not find time to write for *Ruanda Notes*. In a personal letter, she welcomed the news that Miss Ruth Pye-Smith would come from Gahini Girls' School to cover her leave. She wrote to the G.F.S. on Christmas Day 1935, *"Here I am on the eve of leaving for England. I've been longing for my furlough and yet the thought of leaving our bairns is hurting badly, in spite of the fact that I know for 'certain sure' Miss Pye-Smith will do your school a huge amount of good and she'll love and care for your girls as you would yourselves. So why do I fret? Perhaps it is because five years is just too long to keep a right perspective of things, and one lives in the present; as your bairns do when they are playing and it is time for bed. However, I am looking forward with joy and dread to meeting you all; dread because my mind is all dried up and I wonder just what I'll say, so meet me half-way and ask me questions and don't spare me."* She actually departed in March 1936 leaving the School and Miss Pye-Smith "under the Great Headmaster". Europe was in political turmoil and great changes were ahead which would affect the whole world.

Chapter Six
1936 – 1946
PERSEVERANCE: "KEEP ON KEEPING ON"

Miss Hornby's leave in England in 1936

Miss Hornby left Kabale on 10th March and reached Mombasa in time to sail on the *Llansteffan Castle*, one of the Union Castle liners which sailed regularly to England. She arrived there to find a constitutional crisis brewing in her home country. King George V had died in January 1936 and his oldest son Edward was proclaimed as King Edward VIII. The problem was that he wished to marry a divorced lady, Mrs Simpson, and the Constitution would not allow this since he was now the Head of the Church of England. The country was divided, the newspapers full of the crisis. He was never crowned King and chose to abdicate on December 11th 1936 so that he could marry Mrs Simpson. His younger brother George took his place and was crowned King George VI in 1937. This was all going on whilst Miss Hornby was travelling around England visiting the Branches of the Girls' Friendly Society. Wisely, she did not mention the crisis in her letters to her supporters.

Early in 1936 the Secretary of the Girls' Friendly Society, Margaret White, wrote in their magazine that there were 210 names of Dioceses, Branches and subscribers supporting their Own Missionary in Uganda. She asked them to combine for meetings to make Miss Hornby's visits easier. She was to have a holiday from June to August, but would otherwise be on the move from place to place. It must have been an exhausting exercise, meeting so many people in succession, but that was her means of support for God's work. The members were as keen as she was to extend the work in girls' schools in Kigezi and what they called "British Ruanda" (Bufumbira).

Miss Hornby returned across the high seas in December, a stormy passage, and arrived back in Kigezi early in 1937 saying she and her supporters were on an "Allied Adventure". This phrase reflected the political changes which were taking place in Europe that year. She had had a very happy time in England and was most grateful: *"There are such a lot of folk I'd love to thank. England is a wonderful place and everyone is so good and kind . . . Perhaps I looked a bit lost and folks are sorry for me, but it is nice, and I've enjoyed myself. Now I'm going back to our big family in Uganda, rejoicing greatly to carry on for you for a time . . . Ours is an A.A. i.e. Allied Adventure, and it is wonderful when we know that our Ally is Jesus Christ. We must succeed. Let's give Him our very best always."* (9th December 1936)

She left Europe behind with its many problems which would lead to the beginning of the Second World War in 1939. As Chancellor, the Nazi dictator Adolf Hitler was firmly in charge of Germany and already persecuting the Jews. He had a vision of a greatly expanded German Empire and his armies gradually invaded the surrounding countries. His friend Mussolini was in control of Italy and his forces invaded Ethiopia in October 1935 and annexed it in 1936, declaring that African country to be a part of Italy.[1] Germany and Italy were known as the "Axis" powers, while the "Allies" were Great Britain and France.

Balancing School and Village Work

Miss Hornby settled into her normal pattern of school work in term-time and going away on "safari" (or "trek") around the villages of Kigezi in the holidays. She took some weekends in term-time for safari in addition. She wrote in March 1937: *"I found the School in splendid order, but it took me some days to pick up the threads of the work, and after ten months' holiday I found the thirteen hour day made me tired. However I am well away and in my stride again, thanks to you and all your constant backing. I must reduce the Boarding School somehow, for there are 81 girls in it and we have a waiting list of another 14 . . . We are going back to two half-years instead of three terms, because the younger ones find the journey so long. Many of them have a three days' journey, and doing it three times a year means eighteen days' walking. Also, it gives me a longer spell for safari, so we shall break up in June and start in August, carrying on until December."* She did not spare herself, but gave all her strength and efforts to the work which she believed God had given her, namely the discipleship of

---

[1] When Ethiopia fell, the Christian Emperor Haile Selassi went into exile in England. The British organized a counter attack partly from a base in Uganda and liberated Ethiopia after taking Addis Ababa on April 6th 1941. The Emperor was reinstated and the Red Sea route to India, East Africa and the Far East was cleared.

believers in the school and out among the hills of Kigezi. She was like St Paul in her spirit of dedication.[2] Whatever she did, was thoroughly done. She had a good team at the school, including Merabu Nyinenzangi as chief Matron and Keziya Kyirerako, who took Keziya Lugasira's place as second matron when she married in 1935. Then, the second Keziya also became engaged to be married to a teacher. *"That was a nasty blow,"* wrote Miss Hornby, but another reliable girl was chosen, namely Julia Lilian Batembireho. *"I am able to say I have perfect rest as far as the School goes."* (July 1937)

Therefore, she gave herself more and more to the work in the villages, where her heart lay. In the same letter she described a trek near the border of Uganda and Ruanda. *"We now need to ask for a movement amongst the people. As I trek from village to village there seems to be no life. Last Sunday at least 150 came to my camp for a Service, and of that crowd only six could read at all and those badly. I talked to the women and girls after Service in little groups of three and four, but they were absolutely in the dark and sort of hopeless. When one gets up against a crowd like that it is so difficult to make them start to understand sin. They are good living folk. They do not have the sin of drink or impure lives; they are far too lazy to get angry; they have no pride; they don't really know God, so they can hardly be called rebels. It is one of the hardest things to begin to make them understand sin."* As she struggled, she prayed that the Holy Spirit of God would reveal the truth to the people.[3]

Miss Hornby maintained a large semi-permanent house on Rugarama Hill, a spreading bungalow with verandah in the traditional style of the time.[4] She had quite a large "family" sharing the house with her. There is an interesting story about four children whom she brought up as her own. Their father was Andereya Nduluma who was an evangelist working alongside her in the villages of Kigezi and who helped her to set up schools. When their mother died in 1935, he married

---

[2] St Paul gathered the elders of the Ephesian Church and said in his farewell speech, "I do not count my life of any value nor as precious to myself, if only I may accomplish my course and the ministry which I received from the Lord Jesus, to testify to the gospel of the grace of God." Acts 20 v. 24.

[3] See John 16 v. 7-11.

[4] It is now one of the boarding houses for male students at Kigezi High School, adjacent to the School Kitchen. In Miss Hornby's time the area now occupied by the Boys' Dormitories was where Kabale Girls' School was built. See plan of Kabira Station.

MISS HORNBY'S HOUSE ON RUGARAMA HILL WITH THE PRESENT HEADMASTER OF KIGEZI HIGH SCHOOL, MR ELIPHAZ TWINOBUHINGIRO. *[PHOTO: E. TRAILL: 2010]*

again but his new wife did not treat the children well and they were miserable. She did not feed them properly and was cruel to them. Miss Hornby thought so highly of Andereya that she collected the children and took them home with her. One of them, Irene Rosemary (born 28th October 1928) became close to her. The other three were all boys and were fitted into the establishment without difficulty.[5] More will be said about Irene later on.

Miss May Longley, missionary nurse and friend of Miss Hornby, described the Choir of the Girls' School singing carols at the Hospital for Christmas in 1937: *"Doctor and I were doing the evening round, when we suddenly heard a sound of singing. As the sound came nearer we were able to recognise carols . . . As we left one of the wards we caught a glimpse of the singers; they were girls from Miss Hornby's School, and made a very effective picture in their white frocks and carrying lanterns. They sang very sweetly too."*

---

[5]   Source: Edward Bisamunyu: family papers.

As the years went on, more and more girls left the School to be married and this was somewhat disappointing because there were openings for girls to be trained as teachers and midwives. By 1938, Miss Hornby reported, over one hundred girls had been married from the School. She was pleased that they had Christian husbands and she wrote, *"Ninety per cent are leading quiet Christian lives. I think it is a fault that they do not go out preaching and it is mine, for I talk to them very very seriously and say, 'If you are going to walk about the country preaching then don't get married. Your husband, home and your child, if God gives you one, are enough for any woman.' I am sure it is right of course. The glory of being talked about is a great temptation to so many."* (17ᵗʰ September, 1938) She had a great fund of wise advice to give, all based on her observation of human nature and her understanding of her girls.

Revival Times: Changing Lives

Because she had been away on leave and came back into the situation with a fresh mind, Miss Hornby now commented on the Revival in general. In July 1937 she wrote, *"You will have heard of our revival. It is not a mass movement forward but a real sanctification of such a lot of our baptised people. It has been a shock to some of us, for people we thought had been sanctified have confessed to all sorts of sin. They knew that they were wrong and for years have had no peace, but God's Holy Spirit has been working and to Him alone we need to give thanks. The prayers which have been going up for us from England have been and are being answered in a truly wonderful way. Please do not think all our people have been backsliders. Thank God, no, and it is a bit of a comfort, but we praise Him that He has at long last made us see a vision of His holiness."*

In the midst of many blessings, some perplexing situations arose. Miss Hornby told this story: *"In 1935 a girl from another village came to me, as it is part of my work to see all girls and women before they go to the clergy for Baptism. I told her she must wait. Twice more that year she came, and twice more I said, 'No, my child, you've not got there, you've not been converted.' This time she got really angry and tore up her paper and said, 'I'm off to the R.C.s,*[6]* they'll baptise me.' I tried to reason with her, but it was no*

---

[6]   The Roman Catholic Church was also extending its work in Kigezi District at this time. Although not intentional, there was sometimes rivalry between the Churches at village level.

good. I have to confess I came home and forgot about her. Just before I started off on the trek she came to my house, and then I remembered her. She gave me a bit of paper and on it was written badly, 'Please forgive me, Jesus Christ has.' She came in and we sat down to talk about it. She said, 'I went away very, very angry with you and refused to read my Bible or pray. I went to the R.C.'s but it was no good. I was very, very unhappy. Then I settled down and just forgot everything till one day I was in the fields alone working and a voice in my heart said, "You are a bad girl." I said, "No, it is Miss Hornby who is bad. I want to be baptised, she says 'No.'" We argued a long time, and then I went to my hut and found my New Testament. It was dirty and rats had eaten part of it, but I read it, and that night I prayed. At first I was afraid, very afraid, but at last I just called out, "Oh, Jesus, forgive me my anger that crucified Thee." Then I fell asleep. Next day I knew that you have been right and I wrong and that until I met Christ that night I had not been converted, and it was anger. I had always been an angry girl, but I had stopped being angry. When I wanted to be I was not, but the roots were still in my heart and I did not understand I must let Christ dig out those roots. He has done it now, but He hurt me, but I was glad.' That was her story. I said, 'So now you want to be baptised?' 'No,' she said, 'I'm not ready. I have only just begun to know Christ. I have a long way to go.'" Miss Hornby admitted she had not taught the girl or spent much time with her. *"I had not set her on the right road. Christ Himself got her there, but it makes one feel ashamed . . . I want the prayers of the G.F.S. for their own missionary, and for these bairns,[7] for we are living in wonderful times, and some of us are afraid of the wonder of it all."* (July 1937)

Miss Hornby was not the only missionary to feel humbled by the way God was working. A young doctor named Jack Symonds, who was in charge of the Bunyonyi Leper Colony, as it was called then, wrote after a conference at Kisenyi in Ruanda, *"God showed to us something of what full surrender means, and we learned it is not an easy thing to be broken and He requires this of us every day. We learned too, in a greater way than ever before, the possibilities of a life of real fellowship with each other and the Africans . . . Do pray for us as we seek to live out the things which God is revealing to us. It does seem that in these days He is calling out bands of men and women who will be on fire for Him when He returns."* (July 1938)

Another young missionary, Rev. T. Gregory-Smith, had arrived recently to teach at Kigezi High School and administer the other ten boys' schools scattered over Kigezi. He wrote in March 1939, *"It is really grand to come*

---

[7]   Bairns are young children, one of the words Miss Hornby liked to use.

here at a time when the Spirit of God is shaking the place, and to see going on all around the very thing we have been longing to see at home . . . We can only say 'this is the hand of God' . . . Will you pray that I may not stand in God's way and thwart Him?"

A letter from Miss Hornby in the same issue of *Ruanda Notes* makes other points about life at that time: *"Someone said in a letter to me . . . 'What wonderful people you are', and that gave me a nasty jar, for really we are very ordinary people who have the joy of living in a very beautiful part of the world. Our job is as easy as shelling peas compared to some people's . . . Please don't think of us as extraordinary. Our little ones are full of life and up to all sorts of tricks like any other healthy children from seven to eleven years old all the world over. No tree is too hard for them to climb, or water too muddy for them to fall into."*

She questioned the reality of the conversion of a man she met on one of her safaris: *"He said, 'I have been converted and have given up making beer, so now I shall not be able to afford to give you the 3 shillings a year, and the two dresses and a blanket that I used to give you for my child.' But I said, 'The Saza (county) Chief wants men to build a new hospital. If you went to work there you would earn enough in two weeks to supply all the need of your own little girl.' He looked at me as if I had gone mad and said, 'What! You ask me to go and do that sort of work in order to send a girl to school. Certainly not!' I cannot understand it. What does conversion mean to those who believe if it does not enable them to help others younger than themselves who are in such great need?"*

Back in the school, she had a struggle to maintain discipline especially at night when some of the girls wanted to sing hymns and pray at all sorts of times. Some of the other missionaries thought she was being too strict and hard, but she had her reasons and her policy bore fruit in the long term because her girls became stable, disciplined Christian women. *"One teacher who was in charge of the school dining room just came in to meals and then went straight off to sing and pray. If you know anything of a community dining room you can imagine the state it was in, so I said to her, 'Oh Eresi, the girls have not swept or dusted the dining room.' She replied, 'I've no eyes for this world, I see only the things of God.' That sort of thing happened many times a day and went on for two whole weeks. I felt very much inclined, when pay day came, to say to her, 'Of course, you will not want your pay as it is of this world.' However, I did not but I have made it a very strict rule that there is to be no singing at night – all are to be in bed and lights out by 9 p.m."* (July 1939) She also decided not to allow the ring-leaders amongst the girls to return to the school for the next term.

Keziya Kyirerako pops into the story again. She had married a teacher[8] in 1937, much to Miss Hornby's disappointment because she was such a valued member of staff. Her husband, Danieri, was a very quiet man at the time. Later he was converted in the revival and when Miss Hornby visited their village in July 1939 she attended the Church and heard him preach a powerful sermon. *"Afterwards I was talking to the old women and I found his message had got across. Last year his church was almost empty except for Keziya's class of women, and yesterday it was packed. They did not know I was coming and so it was not for me that they came. Danieri has been caught by the revival and is being taught by the Spirit of God, but he has never been in the shouting band."* The last comment suggests that there were some emotional excesses at the time. Miss Hornby continued her village ministry in the school holidays. She stayed in one place where there was a small day school and taught for a week, *"to help to get things straight. They don't seem to have made any progress since I was here in December."*

The beginning of World War Two

The great volcano Nyamulagira erupted early in 1939 causing a red glow in the sky for months in the direction of the Ruanda and Belgian Congo borders. Otherwise, daily life in Kigezi went on normally, but far away in Europe even more momentous events were happening. Hitler's armies invaded Austria in 1938, then marched into Poland in 1939. When he ignored an ultimatum from the British Government requiring his forces to withdraw from Poland, war was declared with Germany on September 3rd, 1939. It became a World War when Japan launched a surprise attack on the American fleet at Pearl Harbour on the island of Oahu, Hawaii, on December 7th, 1941. The Axis powers from then on were Germany, Italy and Japan, against the Allies, namely United Kingdom, France and U.S.A. Fighting took place on many fronts including Ethiopia and North Africa. African soldiers were recruited from Uganda and other countries in the British Empire. The six years of the war had a major effect and precipitated many changes in Africa.

The missionaries at Kabale were very much aware of the growing crisis in world affairs. They attended the Annual Conference for

---

[8] Every village Church had a Catechist or Church Teacher whose work included reading classes. This man was most probably one of these. A Parish would have a number of village Churches within it.

members of Protestant Missions at a centre near beautiful Lake Kivu in July 1939, having fellowship with other missionaries, about 100 in all, and seeking God's guidance. A Mission to Europeans in Kampala was held in August, perfect timing before the War began and many of them were scattered as a result. Dr Joe Church quoted Malachi 3 v. 10 in his letter which called for prayer, *"Prove me now, saith the Lord of Hosts, if I will not open you the windows of Heaven and pour you out a blessing, that there shall not be room enough to receive it."*(20th July, 1939) Miss Hornby noted at the end of 1939, *"We are living in perfect peace in spite of "Old Nasty" and he cannot spoil the Empire."*

The effects of the War on the Mission

The work in Kigezi kept going in all departments, with some restrictions. The price of fuel rose and the postal service was cut back but on the positive side the 250 churches were now virtually self-supporting. It was decided to cut back the medical work at Kabale because the Government was building a new Hospital. There was also a great shortage of drugs. The closure of the Mission Hospital, leaving just the Out Patients' section and a new Dispensary, was a major step after nineteen years of service to the people. The big wards became the dormitories of Kigezi High School Junior Secondary which moved up Rugarama Hill to the site of the Hospital, leaving the Primary section in the buildings in the valley.

The missionaries persevered in their work but some faced major upheaval. Captain Holmes, a member of the Ruanda Mission, was called up and went back to the Army. There was a shortage of funds and so some married couples who went home on leave were advised to stay in Britain for the time being. They were all aware of the great spiritual opportunities in a time of crisis. Mrs Sonia Symonds wrote in July 1939, *"We are among the five married couples who have to stay at home until the money for our passage and support is found. We are not feeling sad, but rejoicing because we know that if God means us to return nothing in the world can keep us back! We are due to sail (D.V.) on September 20th, in the "Dunvegan Castle", with our children John and Betty, so we hope to be seeing you all very soon now. We know you will be praying for us on the boat as we do feel God has given us a message which we long to be faithful in passing on to others."* In actual fact, Dr and Mrs Jack Symonds had a fruitful ministry in England and did not return to Uganda until 1966, when they came back to serve at Kisiizi Hospital in North Kigezi for two years.

The question of the missionaries' annual leave and longer "furlough", as home leave and service was then called, exercised the minds of the Ruanda Council in England. The General Secretary, Mr. Reginald R. Webster, wrote in 1941 that it was not advisable for them to travel home, and anyway passages were very hard to book, and so they could take two months' local leave in Africa when their time of furlough was due. Miss Hornby had a brother in Southern Rhodesia and went to stay with him towards the end of 1942. Some missionaries had health problems and found treatment in South Africa.

In general, it was a time of great resourcefulness. Extra food crops were planted. The people asked, "What can we do to help?" In addition to constant prayers for peace, they wanted to do something practical. Dr Algie Stanley Smith wrote to supporters from Kigeme in Ruanda in September 1941, *"Peace may still be far off, but in mission work as well as in world affairs we need to have 'Peace Aims.' We will be thinking out shortly what we believe God wants us to do here, when 'this tyranny is overpast' – and we will let you fully into our counsels, that we may pray together for the needed grace and the needed supplies for carrying on the 'Holy War' till He comes Whose right it is to reign, the Prince of Peace."*[9]

Changes in Miss Hornby's work, 1940-42

There was exciting news in November 1940 that a fully qualified and experienced teacher, Miss Lilian Clarke, was on the way to Uganda. The Ruanda Mission asked for "a convoy of prayer" for her. It was hoped that she would be allowed to come to Miss Hornby's school in Kabale, but there were some formalities to complete. Her appointment would qualify the School for a Uganda Government grant which would lead to upgrading. Meantime, Miss Hornby wrote to supporters, *"I feel ashamed of myself for living in such peace and comfort while you folks at home are having such a hard time. Actually we have everything very much as usual though prices have gone up. We could put butter on everything if we wanted to.*[10] *Well, at the*

---

[9] One of the C.M.S. War Prayers (1940) says, *"O God, by your Son Jesus Christ you have set on earth a kingdom of holiness to measure its strength against all others; make faith to prevail over fear, and righteousness over force, and truth over the lie, and love and concord over all things, through Jesus Christ our Lord. Amen."*

[10] The missionaries used to make butter at home from the rich milk given by the local breed of small cows. Miss Hornby was not referring to imported butter here, which would be an unobtainable luxury.

end of a year with a qualified staff in the school I find myself as over-run with work as in other years." (November 14th, 1940)

She mentioned two girls, recently confirmed, who would go to Buloba College, Mary Kazhiga and Vanise Bamufunza, and requested prayer that they would grow spiritually. Mary was Miss Hornby's only African Godchild. Fresh from the same College was Eresi Lugasira, sister of Keziya who married in 1935. Eresi had performed very well at College and came top of the class with honours. Miss Hornby said of her, *"She will probably be able to take my place as mistress. I have known her ever since 1923 when as a wee small girlie she started in front of a reading sheet. Now she has passed the Government Primary Teachers' Examination, boys and girls examined together, and has headed the list. Will you please pray for us both that I may not put too much on her."* (Letter undated, some time in 1940.)

Miss Clarke arrived safely in Kampala in March 1941 and to everyone's joy her appointment to Kabale was confirmed. She travelled

A FINE EXAMPLE OF A KIGEZI COW, WITH REV. DAVID AND EVAS TIWANGYE
[PHOTO: E. TRAILL 2010]

twelve hours in a lorry with another missionary, Miss Mildred Forder, and began to settle in. Miss Hornby arranged for her to begin to learn Rukiga immediately. She taught the little English children a few times in their new school, founded in 1940 for missionaries' children and others. It would become Kabale Preparatory School. Miss Lilian Clarke was appointed to serve at Miss Hornby's school which now had 93 girls.

Miss Hornby herself faced a time of transition as her role changed. She wrote with a touch of wistfulness in September 1941, *"I'm on safari, having left your school in the very capable hands of Miss Clarke. I wish you knew her; she will make your school into a proper school. Until now we have just gone along and not done too badly, when I think that in 1922 there was not a Mukiga woman or girl who knew one single letter, or could count up to more than ten. Now there are three Primary Certificated teachers, five elementary Vernacular Certificated teachers and one qualified midwife. You need not be ashamed of your part, for I am sure it is the prayer of the G.F.S. that has kept us going many, many times when I've blundered and made mistakes. Now the trained girls will feel companionship with her who is also a trained teacher. So 'keep on keeping on' praying for them, and your Own Missionary as she tries to get some more work going in the villages."* (29th September 1941) For six months, January to July, Miss Hornby had filled a vacancy for a midwife at the downsized Mission Hospital, while one of her Old Girls, Gertrude Bamwene completed her midwifery training.

The work in the villages continued, described vividly in a letter written in May 1942: *"As I wander round this country I am often very surprised and ashamed of myself when I see the kindness of these people. It never gets into the 'Ruanda Notes' but I know God sees and is not going to let it go unrewarded. For myself I ask your prayers still. I shall be your own missionary just the same, God willing, for another four years or so, but as I see it, it will have to be village work. There is such a lot to be done in the villages, and it is not work that makes a show. One has to go on and on visiting the people in their huts, teaching, seeking those who were once followers of Christ but have gone back, and there are hundreds of them; on this one day I have been to three huts of folks who were once good Christians and they know that they have gone away and left Him and they are finding it so hard to come back. Pray for them, they and we need your prayers. The girls' school meets daily to pray for you all in England."* Miss Hornby's role was clarified in 1943 when she was appointed as Supervisor of Schools for the Anglican Church in Kigezi. That responsibility caused her to go on safari whenever she could, but her skills and wisdom were also needed in other sections of the work of the Mission.

In the same year, the War came to North Africa. General Rommel invaded with the Axis "Afrika Corps" and moved from Libya to Egypt, but the Allies fought back. British forces commanded by Field Marshal Montgomery moved westwards from Egypt and American forces landed in Algiers and pushed eastwards. The "Afrika Corps" was trapped and forced to surrender in May 1943. The team on Rugarama Hill listened to the radio and followed events during the year. Lilian Clarke wrote to supporters on 16th May 1943, *"We rejoice with you in the cessation of hostilities in Africa – it affects you more than it does us."*

A romance on Rugarama Hill

For one couple in particular, the War must have been a distant reality. Festo Kivengere, who was mentioned in Chapter Four when as a ten-year old he first saw Miss Hornby, was now working as a teacher at Kinyasaano Boys' School, Rukungiri. He was a highly gifted and popular teacher but his behaviour in the evenings, including drunkenness, early in 1941 distressed his Headmaster so much that he was on the point of dismissing him. According to Coomes (page 96), he mentioned it when Miss Hornby brought Miss Clarke on her first visit to North Kigezi and decided to allow Festo to stay on. As recorded in his biography, Festo was going through a spiritual struggle, resisting the witness of keen "saved" people (called *"balokole"*) who were enthusiastically sharing their experience of sins forgiven. Even younger members of Festo's family were caught up in the Revival, much to his embarrassment. He finally yielded his life to Jesus Christ in October 1941 and became an evangelist from the day of his conversion, sharing his new faith with the boys in his class the next morning. Two boys were converted through his sincere testimony. He read the Bible avidly and quickly became a member of the preaching teams which went out to the villages at weekends. He visited Kabale from time to time for fellowship and there he renewed a childhood acquaintance with Merabu (or Mera) Nyinenzangi, who was now the Senior African teacher at Kabale Girls' School, under Miss Clarke.

In the summer of 1942, Festo wrote a letter to Mera from Kinyasaano proposing marriage and after some months of prayer and deliberation, she replied accepting him. Their engagement pleased most people who knew them because they were from the same aristocratic Bahororo background and well suited to each other, but Miss Hornby reacted differently. She had formed the opinion that Festo was a rather wild young man and not the right partner for her greatly valued Old Girl and teacher, Mera. (See Coomes page 118) It took her some time to come round, but later she thoroughly approved of the relationship and became a great friend of the family. In December 1942, Festo was transferred to Kigezi High School in Kabale, which made it easier for them to see each other. Their wedding was in St Peter's Church on December 30th 1943 with a hundred guests. Sadly no photographs were taken because of the war-time conditions.

Continuing their story, Festo taught at Kigezi High School until 1945. The words of a visiting missionary from Tanganyika seemed like a "Macedonian call"[11] to Festo and Mera. Possibly they had caught the

THE STATHER HUNT MEMORIAL LEPROSY HOSPITAL ON BWAMA ISLAND, LAKE BUNYONYI. [RUANDA NOTES, C.M.S. ARCHIVES]

---

[11] See Acts 16 v. 9-10 It was Canon Ralph Banks the C.M.S. Education Secretary from Tanganyika who said in St Peter's Church, Kabale, "God has given you revival in Uganda. Have you forgotten all about us in Tanganyika? Can't you come and help us?" (Ref. Coomes p. 133)

spirit of venturesome faith from their mentor Miss Hornby. They offered to go to the Alliance High School in Dodoma, a pioneering adventure for a young Christian teacher with little children. Before leaving, Festo played a full part in the Kabale Convention in December 1945 and spoke at one of the main meetings. They stayed in Tanganyika until 1949 and the story is told in his biography by Coomes.

Work at the Bunyonyi Leprosy Colony

Miss Hornby wrote one of her shortest letters in April 1943, to inform her supporters of her move to Bwama Island in the middle of Lake Bunyonyi. There, hundreds of sufferers from the dread disease of leprosy were treated with love and care by a team led by Dr Len Sharp. Miss May Longley the Nursing Sister was away on sick leave and so Miss Hornby went as a stop-gap. Another missionary, Miss Grace Mash, was in charge of administration and supplies, including the oversight of some fields on the mainland where the patients grew their own food. It must have been a great change from life at the School and from the freedom of her safari work around the villages, but she tackled it with her usual spiritual verve and practical abilities. She wrote, "*Fortunately for the lepers Miss Mash is here and she knows every single leper and all about their homes, clothes, etc. They all love and trust her so the work does not suffer from my lack of knowledge, but we need a nurse. Dr Sharp is really wonderful; his knowledge of leprosy is great, and he is very patient, but it is a nurse's work to carry out his orders. I would not like any of you to see the ulcers on the "morning round" – they are just awful – but you get used even to that. The nurses are fine and do their work well, and they are, of course, themselves lepers. The people seem happy. A Government nurse from Zanzibar visited us and said, 'I suppose it is because it is a Christian colony that they are all so happy. Ours at Zanzibar look so sad, and yet they are well cared-for.' So add Bunyonyi to your prayers, please.*" Over the subsequent Easter weekend Dr Sharp with three Christian leaders from Kabale held a mission on the Island. Miss Grace Mash reported that several people were blessed, the fruits seen in their lives. She continued, "*We do thank and praise God for the way He is helping us all in these days. We have had about twenty new lepers in the last few months. We would ask your prayers for them, as many of them are absolutely heathen. Pray that they may soon know the Saviour as their friend, and share in the Joy and Peace which He gives His children.*" (3rd May, 1943)

In August 1943 Miss Hornby wrote a more explanatory letter about the Leprosy Colony, demonstrating what an "all round" missionary she was, someone who could do good work for the Master in several different professions. She exemplified the three aspects of the Church's mission, namely teaching, preaching and healing.[12] She had been a devoted teacher and educationalist for many years, building up a successful Girls' School. She had also trekked around the District helping to found Churches with little schools attached. Later she had spent months visiting Christians in their homes to teach and encourage them in their new faith. Now, she was putting her whole heart into the work of caring for leprosy patients. She wrote, *"'Bwama' is the name of the island . . . It is a very beautiful spot on a very beautiful lake. It is divided into villages with a hospital and a crèche for untainted children. There are two schools which at the present time are also used for Churches on Sunday. Some of the lepers are not very bad and I could not have said at first that they are lepers. Of course, only the doctor diagnoses, but even after six months, I have learnt a lot. There are over four hundred on the island and some of them are very bad indeed. At first I could not get them out of my mind, I seemed to see them always, but have got used to them now and do not mind so much. I have never been one bit afraid and have worked with them with joy. I believe that if God gives you a job to do He prepares you for it and I can never thank Him enough that He let me do these months here, and made it easy for me too . . . Next month a nurse is coming and then I will go back to the village work. I want to establish two more schools and put in for a Government grant. Pray for this place and for the workers here, and also give thanks for it, for it is being used of God for the winning of many souls, even if their poor bodies are so badly disfigured."*

Although she returned to her educational and pastoral work in the villages, she retained a keen interest in the work on Bwama Island, known as the "Island of Miracles". In January 1944 she reported to her supporters in the G.F.S. that she was on the island again for a fortnight, covering Miss Mash's short holiday. The new nurse was doing great work. *"I am glad I have come,"* wrote Miss Hornby, *"for Miss Thornton seems to have a passion for healing ulcers. I just marvel. In spite of a back injury which prevents her bending, so that she either has to sit on a stool or kneel for two hours at a time on four days a week, she spends the time in the*

---

[12] See, for example, Matthew 9 verses 35-38. The three aspects were sometimes described as the "three legged stool" of Christian missionary work.

wards teaching the dressers how to do the job. I am here as an interpreter but I fear I have fled many times – the smell was so awful – but not so Miss Thornton. She was just lost in her job and it was wonderful to see how the ulcers improved."

Time for Reflection

In the wider world, the Allied forces invaded Italy, making landings at Salerno and Anzio in January 1944. The War was entering its final stages. They pushed northwards and reached Rome on June 4th. Meanwhile the Normandy Landings were being planned. Allied forces landed on the Normandy beaches on June 6th ("D-Day") and then pressed forward across France. The Axis powers were being steadily eroded in Europe but in the area of the Pacific Ocean the Japanese were continuing to fight the Americans.

These events were followed with prayerful interest by people like Miss Hornby who had a wireless set. Otherwise, work in Kigezi continued peacefully. The agricultural landscape was changing, although traditional methods of strip-cropping with bunding[13] had been quite commonly practised to stop soil being washed away. J.W. Purseglove was the very active District Agricultural Officer from 1944 until 1952. According to Carswell, he learned Rukiga and introduced the *"Plani Ensya"* (New Plan) to terrace the hills systematically,[14] working through the chiefs. It was a "carrot and stick" approach, with rewards such as prizes for progress in soil conservation in sub-counties (*Gomborora*). There was also a certain amount of discipline through local courts to deal with detractors who refused to alter their ways. Courses were run for the chiefs to learn new methods to teach the people. It was a successful means of controlling soil erosion on the steep slopes and has endured until the present day. Miss Hornby with her eye for order and symmetry would have approved of the policy and must have observed whole hillsides being transformed from patchy cultivation

---

[13] Bunding in this context meant lines of stones and weeds piled at the bottom of plots as a measure to prevent the loss of soil by sheet erosion and gullying during heavy rainfall. It was a traditional practice, modified and improved by the Agricultural Department.

[14] The angle of slopes was measured, those steeper than 20 degrees were taken out of cultivation. Slopes up to 15 degrees were to have terraces 16 yards wide. Steeper slopes had narrower terraces.

into carefully terraced and productive land. Her many women and girls in the villages must have worked very hard.

Miss Hornby took Miss Clarke on a safari to see the village schools in action. The Kabale Girls' School was doing well under her leadership. *"She is very wise about all school work and has made your school into a proper one"*, wrote Miss Hornby, *"We had an 'Old Girls' reunion on 31ˢᵗ December and seventy-two came. It was good to see them all again and to realize that badly as I've done the job for you, under God's grace and thanks to all your prayers, many are truly converted and are wonderful Christians."* (January 1944) She did not try to hold onto the work at the school, but moved on as God guided her.

It was Miss Hornby's 60ᵗʰ year, and she seems to have been in a reflective mood. She went back to work on Bwama Island and wrote, *"Once again I am doing holiday work at this Leper Colony. 'Your Own Missionary' certainly leaves you guessing as to what she will do next. But now, I think, I am almost settled until I come home. I want to stay (D.V.)[15] until the end of 1946 or the beginning of 1947, when I shall have completed ten years this tour and thirty in the field. If all is well I am going to work here for the next year while Miss Mash goes on leave, so you will hear something of Bunyonyi in the future. I must, with your help, readjust my life to life on a Leper Island, so pray that I may have wisdom in all things. It is not altogether new to me, for I have worked here on and off for ten months and know all the workers and lots of the people themselves. Nevertheless it is up to you to see that I do it for His sake . . . Pray for me as I carry on with the job that seems to be the one I am meant to do until I come home."* (25ᵗʰ August, 1944)

Revival Problems

Miss Hornby was present in Kigezi all through the beginnings and the years of the expansion of the East African Revival. As noted in Chapters Three, Five and Six, she encountered many problems as she attempted to teach women and girls how to live Christian lives of integrity. She found that new Christians could talk and sing a lot, often noisily and using all the right words, but they found the matter of following Christ's teaching in daily life much more

---

[15] D.V. is the abbreviation for the Latin *'Deo Volente'* meaning 'God Willing' (Concise Oxford Dictionary, 1959).

difficult. She was humble in her own approach, realising that God Himself was at work in wonderful ways. She maintained strict discipline in the Girls' Schools and encouraged Bible reading and prayer. Her wisdom and common sense were sought sometimes by the leaders of the Revival when major problems arose as the movement spread far and wide in East Africa. There is a reference to her in a letter written by Festo Kivengere to a friend in December 1944. A meeting was called by African leaders to consult with Dr Len Sharp on the subject of "walking in the light" and Miss Hornby was present.[16]

Miss Mary Sharp, daughter of Dr Len Sharp, recalled an incident: *"Miss Hornby was very wise in how she answered people and taught the Scripture truths. Sometime in the 1940s/1950s she was challenged by the brethren as to why she had not been confessing her sins publicly at meetings. She explained using Scriptures, how when she had sinned she sought to confess to God quickly. He kept His word and forgave her sins. (I John 1 v. 9) And God says, 'I am He that blotteth out thy transgressions for mine own sake and will not remember thy sins.' (Isaiah 43 v. 25) Praise God! So how could she at a meeting later bring sins God had forgiven and forgotten to public attention again?"* We do not know how the leaders of the Church responded to Miss Hornby on those occasions, but it would have been with grace and gentleness.

Dr Joe Church in his autobiographical account of the Revival says, *"It must be remembered that the road to revival is a dangerous road and we must expect cunning and sometimes terrible attacks from the world, the flesh and the devil."*(*Quest for the Highest*, p.254f.) He lists a number of contrary trends which arose as the message of Revival penetrated the different societies and cultures in East Africa. Some became jealous of the leadership. Others strove for acceptance through outward signs such as weeping or public confession of gross sins. A number of newly-revived Christians claimed a "once for all" experience which meant that they did not have to exercise daily discipline in their lives. In the West Nile District in the North of Uganda there were "Trumpeters" who preached loudly through megaphones on all possible occasions. Some others pursued a false orthodoxy, copying different practices instead of exercising a

---

[16] Letter to Dr Ralph Leech, quoted in letter to the author, 8th September, 2009.

redemptive faith. Many grew cold by placing tribal loyalty above obedience to Christ. Another common trend was the thoughtless singing of hymns and choruses, the Luganda *"Tukutendereza Yesu"*[17] in particular. Certain words, such as "broken-ness", frequently used by preachers, could become meaningless "jargon" which was very sad. Lastly, legalism arose through the Re-Awakening *(Okuzukuka)* Movement in Buganda and caused a big split in the whole Revival movement. Miss Hornby lived through these times and observed all these trends and more besides. In her letters she did not often comment on what she saw. She kept on doing her best in her work and encouraging others to walk with the Lord Jesus day by day.

Dr Joe Church's book ends with a positive description of real Revival and what it can and does mean in the lives of thousands of Christians not only in East Africa but around the world as the message spread: *"The characteristics of these fellowships can be summarised: Love of the brethren – Confession of sin – Willingness to be challenged and to challenge – Concern for the lost and bereaved – Team witness – Freedom in prayer and preaching – Wanting light and openness – Lack of embarrassment between the races – Joy, singing and laughter –and lastly the safety of homes where Christ dwells, and He is seen in people's faces."* (Page 259) Dr Ralph Leech who served at Mengo Hospital and Maseno Hospital in Kenya from 1938 – 1964 wrote recently, *"I have been quite moved by going through a collection of some 150 personal letters written to Bertha and myself from brethren all over East Africa – African and European – in those days. They give a wonderful sense of the immediacy of the Lord in all our little daily affairs – across all racial and social divides (as well as 'on the spot' comments on events and situations as they arose) and it was all because we were so conscious of our common position before God as sinners saved by the blood of Jesus, so costly."* (Letter, 8th September 2009) So it was and so it can be. Miss Hornby would join her sincere testimony to all those features of real revival and she carried the light of Jesus in her until her dying day.

---

[17] See Appendix Two for the words of this song which became the theme song of the East African Revival.

Chapter Seven
1946 – 1966
"REACHING OUT FOR WHAT LIES AHEAD, I PRESS TOWARDS THE GOAL"

Immediately after the War

Miss Hornby was in her senior years. In her youth she was nicknamed "Nyakaishiki" (the young girl) but latterly she became known as "Kaaka (grandma) Hornby". According to Margaret Oliver (nee Burt), she also had a nickname "Kamagamaga", meaning "Like a little bird" because she walked and talked so quickly. She seems to have contemplated retirement in England after 30 years in Uganda (letter August 1944 already quoted). In the 1960s she told us a story that she wrote a proposal to the C.M.S. after the War ended but was told, "It is against the Regulations." A bit of a rebel at heart, she sent back a telegram, "Change the Regulations, I'm coming!" However, whatever her scheme was, she changed her mind. She chose to take her much needed leave with members of her family in southern Africa. She realised that Africa was truly her home and her Lord and Master had more work for her to do there.

Seeing a need, she offered to cover Miss Mash's leave for the year 1945 at the Leprosy Settlement, relying as ever on the prayers of the faithful G.F.S. members. Writing in June 1945, Dr Len Sharp paid tribute to her work, *"She has been giving herself with untiring and unselfish devotion to this always exacting field of work."* Relief came with the arrival of two Nursing Sisters from England, Marguerite Barley and Janet Metcalf, but they needed to spend some months in Kabale learning the language before they could work on the Island. Janet wrote after four visits to the Island: *"It is a most beautiful spot, but there is a mass of work waiting to be done. Having been so long without a Sister, the hospital boys, who are all lepers themselves, have no idea of nursing; and we were upset to see the poor deformed people come up, take off their own dressings, be handed a clean one without any attempt to clean the wound, and then be left to bandage themselves up, even when the leprous ulcer was in a most inaccessible place, like the top of an arm. The very worst dressings are done by Miss Hornby herself, but with all the rest of the work of the island, she could not possibly watch them all . . . Please pray for the people over there. The Christian lepers are a wonderful experience as they praise Him in their weakness and suffering: but many do not yet know the Lord and their dull apathy is pitiful to see."* (19th June, 1945)

When Miss Mash returned and the two Nurses moved to the Island, Miss Hornby went to South Africa on leave for some months in 1946. Possibly her family circumstances had changed, leaving her without a home base in England. We know she had a brother in Southern Rhodesia and her older sister, Lucy Mary, was bound for a teaching post in South Africa before the First World War (see Chapter Two) but the whereabouts of her family have not been revealed in our researches. Perhaps contact will be made with her relations as a result of publishing this book.

When Miss Hornby returned to Kabale from South Africa towards the end of 1946, she offered to cover Miss Clarke's leave by assuming responsibility for the Girls' Boarding School once again. It was very difficult for the missionaries to book passages to Britain after the War because the demand was so great. Gradually they all left Kabale for their much-needed "furlough". Miss Hornby was left as the Senior Missionary on Rugarama Hill and also responsible for all the 35 schools in the District. It must have been quite a load, but she kept it up. *"If all is well, Miss Clarke should be back in September to start the third term; if not, I'm afraid it won't start. If I had a full staff it would be easy, but, with all the help I do get, I am teaching full time and I am in charge of the schools in the District as well. I love that job; the children are all so keen and give me such a welcome. Some of the girls there still wear cow-hides and these make their work very dirty during sewing lessons. So I take out bits of cloth for them to put under their sewing to keep it clean. Little by little we are getting fewer wearing skins in our schools and we hardly ever see a boy in school in one . . . We have had a very happy year so far."* (11th June, 1947)

It is not surprising that her services were known and recognised by the Government. In the New Year Honours List for 1948 she was awarded the M.B.E.[1] for her services to African Education but she did not go back to England to receive it. She would have seen it as a tribute to her colleagues and her girls. In fact, this later part of her life story until her death in 1972 should be written by them. Use will therefore be made of the many letters and comments collected during our research amongst those who knew her very well indeed.

---

[1] The initials M.B.E. stand for Member of the Order of the British Empire.

Miss Hornby's last phase of active service from 1947 onwards carries an aura of fulfilment. Again she became the Supervisor of the schools in Kigezi District founded by the Anglican Church, back in village work amongst the people who loved her and whom she regarded as her own. Her old students were scattered in the villages, many setting a Christian example in their homes and families and some involved in the work of teaching literacy, arithmetic and basic education in village schools. Some had married clergy and church teachers, sharing in their ministry.

The Silver Jubilee of the Ruanda Mission 1921 – 1946

At this historic juncture, those involved in the Mission both at home and in Africa consciously looked back with thanksgiving over the events and progress of their first twenty-five years. A special Jubilee edition of *Ruanda Notes* was compiled and Miss Hornby wrote a short article:

"As I look at these people today and try and remember what my feelings were when I arrived here in March 1923, I feel rather like 'Alice through the looking glass.' I remember the awful feeling of 'just how can one start on the great crowd of ignorant people?' There was just nothing to work with and no means of getting anything, but God provided and still does. I quickly went on safari with Dr and Mrs Sharp into Bufumbira and after four whole weeks we were able to get four little girls who were allowed by their parents to come to school, and that started the school. Next safari was with Dr and Mrs Stanley Smith when we brought back five more. Of those nine, five have now got children either in the school or being trained for teachers or nurses; two have died; two have only boys. In a very short time we had a school established, that is thirty-six girls, and Miss Attlee of Toro sent us a teacher and a matron. In six months eleven girls could read, and they had to take their turn with teaching others.

"In 1929 we had three outside classes with fifty or more in each, but everything was so simple: grass hut, reading sheets, and sand for learning to write. Yet out of that, in twenty-three years has grown a full Primary School with old girls as fully qualified teachers and over one hundred and sixty girls and four Primary Village Schools, also staffed with old girls as qualified teachers. Some twenty girls are away now being trained as teachers, nurses or midwives. I know there is much we would like to cover up, but last year I spent eight months on safari and saw a lot of homes of old married girls, very many of them are truly clean Christian homes and I thank God for them. He in His mercy has over-ruled my many mistakes, and there are a lot of really truly Christian girls and women workers or wives." (14th December, 1945)

How the girls remembered her

To confirm Miss Hornby's account, we have the testimony of two of the pioneer girls who came from Kisoro in 1923. Mrs Eseza Bisagavu was aged four at the time and regarded Miss Hornby as "our mother". She remembers that she dressed neatly and was a vegetarian. She habitually read the Bible and prayed. She taught the Catechism. She loved singing hymns, No. 236 in today's *Runyankore/Rukiga Hymn Book* being one of her favourites. Below are the words in English from the *Golden Bells* hymn book which she would have used:

Jesus loves me! This I know,
For the Bible tells me so;
Little ones to Him belong,
They are weak, but He is strong.
    Yes, Jesus loves me,
    Yes, Jesus loves me,
    Yes, Jesus loves me,
    The Bible tells me so.

Jesus loves me! He who died
Heaven's gate to open wide;
He will wash away my sin,
Let His little child come in.

Jesus loves me! Loves me still
When I'm very weak and ill;
From His shining throne on high
Comes to watch me where I lie.

Jesus loves me! He will stay
Close beside me all the way;
If I love Him, when I die
He will take me home on high.

No. 661 in *Golden Bells* **(1925 edn)**

MRS ESEZA BISAGAVU AGED 87 WITH HER FAMILY IN DECEMBER 2006.
[PHOTO E. TRAILL]

They are typical of the person Miss Hornby was, and are a summary of the message she came to Africa to share. Lastly, Eseza comments that the girls behaved responsibly and there were no drop-outs because of immorality.

Eseza's friend, Mrs Miriam Serucaca recounted her memories to her daughter-in-law, Mrs Margaret Turimumahoro. She said she was one of the first girls from Kisoro in 1923. The girls all loved Miss Hornby. She taught them cooking and sewing table cloths and even how to make a bra. They baked cakes in sufurias[2] with sand in the bottom and charcoal on the lid. Miriam said that the girls co-operated very well in the early days. She also described how she and her husband-to-be walked over the hills from Kisoro to Kabale for their wedding in St Peter's Church in the 1930s. (Interview, October 2008.)

Five other ladies[3] took part in our research in 2002 by completing questionnaires. They could remember Miss Hornby at different stages in the first 25 years of the school. When all the different scraps of information about Miss Hornby are put together, they reveal a consistent Christian life with cleanliness, godliness, discipline and concern for the needy as its hallmarks. Several mention her quick footsteps and the way she mixed up Luganda and Runyankore/Rukiga.

Merabu Kivengere told us that she frequently exclaimed to the assembled girls, "*Abaffe! Naayanga!*" In English the meaning would be, "Friends!" (Lug.) "I refuse!" (Ruk.) Evidently, this saying caused general amusement, possibly because the word *abaffe* in Rukiga is close to *abafiire* referring to the dead, causing the schoolgirls to giggle at her mistake. As for strict discipline, Merabu remembered that girls were not allowed to wear sweaters when working because they might become lazy. Miss Hornby wanted them to work very hard. She taught them to sing but was not a good singer herself. She read the Bible regularly but did not lead Bible studies and never preached in Church. She visited the poor, looked after orphans and widows. In this way, she showed her love for God. Merabu regretted that no records or photos of the school survived because Miss Hornby thought they were not necessary and had burnt them when she left. She was camera-shy. Merabu concluded, "*She travelled all over Kigezi looking for girls to educate – walking on foot! She*

---

[2]　A sufuria is a type of large saucepan with a projecting flat rim but no handle, usually made of aluminium.

[3]　Their names, with the year of joining the School, are: Canon Merabu Kivengere (1927), Mrs Mirieri Katarikaawe (1937), Mrs Florance Byabamazima (1937), Mrs Catherine Buregyeya (1940), Mrs Kellen Beyeeza (1948). We are very grateful for all the information given by these ladies, also to Canon Peter Rwabyoma for translating the Rukiga scripts of the Questionnaires into English.

should be remembered as a good example of loving God. She dedicated her life to serving Him. She was a hard worker, extremely selfless."(Interview 23rd November, 2002.)

Mrs Mirieri Katarikaawe was impressed by the way Miss Hornby taught younger and older girls together. She really loved the girls. She worked closely with the churches and her behaviour exuded faith in God. The social benefits were great because formerly the Bakiga did not believe that girls could go out and be employed. Mirieri concluded, *"God kept her and gave her a long life to see the girls she taught get employment. She felt happy to see the results of her labour among the girls she taught."* (Interview 5th August, 2002)

Mrs Catherine Buregyeya remembered the discipline of hard work. *"The girls woke up early to dig. They produced their own food. Miss Hornby never allowed a girl to wear a torn dress. It had to be mended."* (Interview in 2002, no date given.)

Mrs Florance Byabamazima remembered the special dormitory started in 1937 for the youngest girls (Kindergarten) and how Miss Hornby used to check the girls at bedtime every evening. In the same year, she bought a car and used it for the long safaris out to the villages. (Handwritten undated notes, 2002.)

Mrs Kellen Beyeeza told us about the results of Miss Hornby's work in the school. *"She liked her school girls to behave very well. Her girls looked especially clean, unlike the rest. The students she taught are still useful in Uganda and very responsible even today. They even behave differently from others."* (Interview 9th May, 2002)

The post-War Rush for Education

Miss Hornby would not spend much time in looking back when there was work to be done. Although she had many responsibilities in Kabale, her heart was in the villages. In 1946 she wrote a most interesting letter to the Girls' Friendly Society which did not appear in the Mission magazine. It was entitled "Fellowship" and described the strong bond between the G.F.S. members in England and the girls who were receiving rudimentary education in the remote villages: *"A group of girls is going to one of the village reading huts where there is a girl teacher. The village is on the borders of the Belgian Congo and away from the motor road . . . The G.F.S. support a missionary in Uganda. The Uganda Fund started many years ago for pioneer work among women and girls in the Kigezi District. The G.F.S. has faithfully supported the work by prayers and money. There are now a fine girls' boarding school, a training school for native teachers and five village schools run by girl teachers. It is to one of these schools that this group of girls is going. Eseza[4] is an old boarding school girl. She started to work in one of the faraway villages. Four girls were then being taught in the village reading hut by the man teacher. Three weeks later she had thirty-six girls and young women coming four days a week. This meant five classes and she was the only teacher, so she had to make her class teach and then she taught those she had been teaching. Only four could read, but in a short time there were many more. But to work up this school she had to spend hours and hours in visiting. Sometimes people were rude to her and told her to go away, but slowly they came to realise that she only wanted the girls for a few hours every day and that she was one of their people. Now girls in distant villages far away go to learn how to write and sew as well as read. You G.F.S. hold in your hand all the girls' and women's work in this part of Uganda, and are touching and helping hundreds of girls in the neighbouring country of Ruanda . . ."* (Article in the G.F.S. Magazine, May 1946.)

Miss Hornby went on to describe the Boarding School, the Day School and the small Training School for village teachers. Thinking back to her own school days as described in Chapter One, she had adopted Victorian methods including the model of the Pupil Teacher system for the rapid expansion of basic education based on Christian teaching. In the system devised by Miss Hornby all the girls learned from the Bible and had the opportunity to prepare for baptism and confirmation. It was a significant movement within the general rush for education which swept through Uganda after the War. Miss Hornby attributed the success in Kigezi to the G.F.S. *"The new school is a beautiful place and teaching in it is a real pleasure. We can have drill in the central hall, while the four classrooms carry on with other lessons. It is a delightful airy building. There are six teachers, all old girls who have grown up in the school. They are young but they do splendid work. It is wonderful how a girl holds down her job if she is put in a position of responsibility. We realise why it is. It is because of G.F.S. backing. The school stands for G.F.S. All of us who know what these letters mean and are ready to carry on and do our best cannot fail even if we make mistakes. Behind us are so many branches at home. It is a strong chain . . ."* (G.F.S. Magazine, May 1946)

---

4   It is possible that Eseza the teacher mentioned here is the same person as the one who helped us in our research in 2002 and is still living in Kabale.

Miss Hornby at home and "on safari"

Miss Hornby now stayed in a house half way up Rugarama Hill as the base for her work. Two young missionaries about to start their first tour in Ruanda had a remarkable encounter with her in 1950. Mabel Jones and Heather Osborn were on the last leg of the long journey from Kampala, travelling in an elderly lorry grinding up the Hill late at night. *"We were very late and just before we reached the first house we saw a figure in her housecoat pointing to the top of the hill and shouting, 'Don't stop. Keep going right on to the top.' She had been asleep, 1 a.m., when she heard the lorry's weary engine. She thought it might be difficult for the driver to start again if it stopped at her house. To us 'raw recruits' it was like the voice of a prophet, a voice of encouragement. So we continued."* (Mabel Jones, Questionnaire, August 2002)

Being the Supervisor of thirty-five schools in the District took Miss Hornby out amongst the people of Kigezi. She travelled far and wide on the rough stony, dusty or muddy roads and tracks over the hills and along the valleys in her sturdy car. She was still the "Own Missionary" of the Girls' Friendly Society and wrote frequently to thank the members for their support. *"It is many years since you started supporting me as your Own Missionary and things have changed very much. Your 'little girls' are now married women with children growing up. Agenesi, known by name to some of you, is the mother of six children and the wife of one of the new deacons[5] – in fact, the wives of all those deacons are your old girls and all truly out and out for Christ. Yes, my friends, you can thank God, our Father; He has heard your prayers and many, many have been converted because of your faithfulness."* She went on to explain that her work covered both the boys' and the girls' schools in the District, but she would have loved to concentrate on the women and girls. *"Last year, I travelled nearly 3,000 miles inspecting schools and I see so much I'd like to do that is not school supervision. I'm always sad I cannot do more, for the children do love you to be with them. It's bad for me, but I get such a welcome everywhere; the children come up to my camp and just watch me – bless them. They love to see my camp bed being put up or taken down and, when I start my gramophone, life is not easy or quiet – they just love it!"* (16th June, 1949)

All the time, the steady work of discipleship was going on. Miss Hornby was conscious that people coming out of ignorance and darkness needed to be taught the truth from God's Word, but how could

---

[5]   Agenesi was married to Rev. K. Kasisiri (see photo opposite).

this be done if they had no Bibles in their own language? In March 1950 a consignment of 3,060 Bibles in Runyoro (the language of Bunyoro in North-West Uganda) arrived in Kabale and the copies were sold quickly. Runyoro is a close relative of Runyankore-Rukiga amongst Bantu languages, but with differences.[6] She asked her supporters, *"Please*

ORDINATION GROUP AT KABALE, 6 FEB. 1949
[RUANDA NOTES, C.M.S. ARCHIVES]

LEFT TO RIGHT:

REV. ERIYA NDYANABO (PRIESTED) AND HIS WIFE, GLADISI

REV. KEZEKIYA KASISIRI (DEACON) AND HIS WIFE, AGENESI

REV. SEDURAKA GALEBA (DEACON) AND HIS WIFE, EPHRASI

REV. ERENESITI RUTAGARUKAYO (DEACON) AND HIS WIFE, ESETERI

REV. KEZERONI MURANGA (DEACON) AND HIS WIFE, EPHRASI

REV. ANDEREYA GIHANGA (DEACON) AND HIS WIFE, GLADISI

---

6   A report in *Ruanda Notes* (1952) indicates that the Rukiga Hymn book was joyfully received in that year and work on the shortened Rukiga Prayer Book was in progress. Translation is a slow process.

pray very, very much that each Bible may be read and that God's Holy Spirit may instruct each reader, for truly so few of our people really know the Scriptures." In the same month Bishop Aberi Balya, the saintly Bishop of Fort Portal, came to St Peter's Church, Kabale, for a big Confirmation Service at which there were 300 candidates. Miss Hornby observed that they needed prayer, that it would be a meaningful event in their Christian lives. Thinking back to her youth,[7] she wrote, *"I don't know what you think about confirmation, but my confirmation day was a great day; now I'm very old I still remember what Christ taught me then."* (27th March, 1950)

Miss Hornby certainly made good use of every opportunity for sharing the Gospel, using the simple technology of the day. *"If all is well, I'm going out to one of our furthest district churches for Easter. I'll be away a week, taking my lantern and gramophone and hope to have a children's service on Easter Day, expecting about 200 of them, and a lantern service on Friday, Saturday and Sunday. At Christmas, Lilian Clarke and I went to another district for the same thing. We expected 90 to 100 children and had 100 old Christmas cards for them, but over 300 came, so we dared not give out the cards. We had prepared a service for one hour but the children refused to go and we were with them over two hours – then we refused to stay! It's no joke carrying on moment by moment – at least I find it a great strain. Do you think Christ ever felt anxious? No, I expect He lived so near to His Father that nothing was ever amiss."* (27th March, 1950)

Development of Teacher Training for Women

Miss Hornby observed the changes in Uganda and supported the developments in educational policy. As early as 1944, Max Warren,[8] the General Secretary of C.M.S., had written prophetically in the *C.M.S. Newsletter* that educated Africans would be seeking, *"partnership, not condescension, paternalism or colonialism"* after the War. (No. 54, Sept. 1944) He stressed the importance of teacher training and held Uganda up as an example of co-operation between the Church and the Government more developed than anywhere else in Africa. (No. 55, Oct. 1944)

Miss Hornby always treated everyone alike. Her persevering, long-term educational work of leading women and girls into new freedom

---

[7] Constance was confirmed at St Mary's Church, Twickenham, in 1902. (See Chapter Two.)

[8] Canon Max Warren was a brother of the late Rev. Jack Warren, and uncle to Miss Sheelagh Warren.

and dignity was a part of a much wider picture. She had always helped her learners to become the teachers of those who came after them, and so it was a natural development to look beyond the Girls' School with its small training school and to develop a full Vernacular Teacher Training Centre in Kabale, with the support of the Church and the Protectorate Government.

Miss Margaret Clayton arrived in Kabale in 1948 to be the Headmistress of the Girls' School. She remembered Miss Hornby as *"small and slight and bird-like. She moved and spoke quickly."* (Questionnaire, August 2002.) Her coming released Miss Lilian Clarke for the work of setting up the new Centre. Rooms in the Divinity School were used and it opened in January 1948. About twelve girls were admitted each year for a three-year Course, with instruction in the local language, encompassing academic studies and practical skills, needlework and domestic science. By 1952 the Centre had become well-established and accredited by the local Government, but its time was limited. The Protectorate Government under Sir Andrew Cohen decided to re-organise the teacher training system in 1953. The entrance qualifications would be raised and English would henceforth be the medium of instruction. The number of teacher training colleges would be reduced from 41 to 23.

It was sad that the "V.T.T.C.", as it was called, had to close. Miss Clarke had written about the all-round success of the Centre: *"We do praise the Lord that both our African staff members are keen Christians and very dear girls. The students, too, are going ahead, spiritually and academically, and there is a real atmosphere of reverence and a hunger for spiritual things amongst them. We praise for some who have given their lives to Him, especially one who gave a lively witness and made a stand for the Master at our Girl Crusader Camp in August."* (13th September, 1950) On leave in England in 1952 she continued: *"About forty girls are trained over a period of three years. An average of twelve qualified teachers, with the Government's Education Department certificates, pass out yearly to teach the children of Kigezi and Ankole . . . The girls work really hard to attain the standards which are required of them before they can be qualified . . . They are encouraged to attain a high standard in academic subjects, in their handwork and needlework, in domestic science subjects, physical training and community work, firstly to the glory of His Name . . . In community work last year they made collection-trays, blue kneelers for the Communion rail, and embroidered white cloths for the Communion tables, and these gifts were handed to the Rural Deans of Ankole and Kigezi for distribution amongst some of their churches . . . Government reports of the Centre have been quite satisfactory and the students have passed their examinations with better credit than we expected . . . The Centre's motto is: "The truth shall make you free."* (8th April, 1952)

When Miss Clarke returned from her year on leave in England, she had the hard task of closing down the Centre which she had built up only a few years before. In December 1954 the girls from the V.T.T.C. left Kabale to join the College at Mbarara. By a special arrangement in 1955 twenty different girls and young women came for a one-year teaching course under Miss Clarke, sited within Kabale Girls' School. Some came straight from primary school, others had been working in church schools. All did well in their final examinations. In 1956 she became the Schools Supervisor of the 35 Government-aided Primary schools, taking over from Miss Hornby and Rev. T. Gregory-Smith. The missionaries were remarkably resilient and adaptable. With good grace they embraced changes and moved on, often undertaking roles for which they had no special training but keeping spiritually close to Jesus and to one another in the revival fellowship of Africans and Europeans.

FAREWELL PARTY GIVEN TO MISS HORNBY BY SOME OF THE OLD GIRLS OF KABALE SCHOOL *[PHOTO: BETTY THOMSON FEB. 1954]*

LEFT TO RIGHT:
ERINORA (ONE OF THE FIRST GIRLS AND MOTHER OF THE LITTLE GIRL IN FRONT)
MARY (DAUGHTER OF AN OLD GIRL AND MOTHER OF PATRICK, IN FRONT OF MISS HORNBY)
AGENESI, WIFE OF THE REV. K. KASISIRI AND FORMER MISTRESS
BLANDINA, THE FIRST GIRL AND LATER SCHOOL MATRON

Sadness followed by a very special Royal visit

While Miss Hornby was continuing her work amongst the hills of Kigezi, people all round the world were saddened to hear of the death of King George VI on February 6th, 1952. He and Queen Elizabeth were loved deeply and respected by all their peoples. They had made several visits to Empire and Commonwealth countries during the times of peace before and after the Second World War. Their elder daughter, Princess Elizabeth, aged 25, was on a visit to Kenya with her husband Prince Philip Mountbatten en route to Australasia. They were staying at "Treetops" on Mount Kenya, when the news of the King's death broke. At once arrangements were made for them to return to England. They flew first to Entebbe to connect with a flight to London. *"Entebbe Airport was dark and dismal that night; thunderstorms crashed and echoed around the turbulent waters of Lake Victoria; the rain beat piteously down. On the deserted tarmac stood a solitary aircraft, waiting to take the young Queen home to her sorrowing people."* ("The Royal Visit to Uganda 1954", p. 4)

A long period of mourning followed, but tears turned to joy as preparations were made for the Coronation of Queen Elizabeth II on June 2nd 1953. From the start she took her responsibilities to the Commonwealth very seriously. At the end of 1953 she and Prince Philip embarked on a five month tour of Commonwealth countries. Uganda was one of the last to be visited, but the three days they spent there must have been amongst the happiest times of the tour. Queen Elizabeth II and Prince Philip arrived at Entebbe on April 28th, 1954 in the morning. They stayed at Government House in Entebbe and the Welcome Ceremony was held there, followed by an Investiture and Garden Party to which 5,000 guests from all over Uganda had been invited. The second day should have been spent in Kampala but there was a poor security situation with neighbouring Kenya which curtailed the arrangements. The planned ceremonies took place in Entebbe in the morning then they flew to Jinja to open the Owen Falls Dam and Hydroelectric Power scheme. It was a spectacular event when the waters of the Nile were held back exposing the rocks below the dam and then released by the Queen: *"An unaccustomed silence fell. Then, after the speeches, Her Majesty pulled a switch raising the sluices and the waters of Lake Victoria surged through in a stupendous current. Spray rose to a hundred feet, gleaming blue and white in the sunlight, as the river resumed its long and tortuous journey to the Mediterranean."* (*Ibid.*, page 16) After the ceremony, they flew back to

Entebbe for the night. On the third day, April 30th, they visited the Western Province and Miss Hornby had her chance to see the Queen.

Miss Hornby was given a farewell party by some of her Old Girls. She was due to go on leave to England but, as her Retirement Minute in the C.M.S. records states,[9] the date was delayed for a month so that she could be presented to the Queen. With nothing smart to wear after so many years, she borrowed a small black hat, long black gloves and a small handbag from a young missionary fresh out from England, Miss Betty Bromilow. In her own words Miss Hornby gave a vivid account of probably the most thrilling moment of her life: *"My last day in the Western Province of Uganda, 30th April, I had the great honour of seeing Her Majesty Queen Elizabeth. It was a really blazing day. As we waited I found a little shade and felt so sorry for the great crowd of people waiting with no shade on the side of Lake Edward for one whole hour. We watched the motor-launch come across the Lake; the Queen had been having lunch in the National Park and had been seeing the animals there. As her launch pulled out, twelve canoes met her and formed a guard of honour, six on each side. It was a wonderful sight, with all the paddles in perfect time. At the landing stage, she was met by the Mukama (King) of Bunyoro, a fine tall man in his beautiful blue and gold state-robes. He walked with her to the shelter which had been built native fashion of reeds; the ground was covered with heads of papyrus, with lion, leopard and monkey skins in the shelter. Mats made by Africans of palm leaves were used instead of a red carpet for her to walk on from the boat. Everything was from the country, and I was glad that we could entertain Her Majesty and the Duke without any aid from Britain. There were seven of us to be presented, four Africans and three British. It was a great honour. I've never, never thought it could be mine; I was overcome and felt so unworthy. I was able to watch Her Majesty for twenty-five minutes with no one or anything else in between."* (Written in England, 5th July, 1954)

The Queen and Prince Philip returned to Entebbe for the last hours of their visit. That night they flew to Tobruk in Libya where the newly launched Royal Yacht "Britannia" was waiting for them. On board were Queen Elizabeth the Queen Mother and their two children, Prince Charles aged five and Princess Anne aged four, for a family reunion after five long months. The visit to Uganda had been an unqualified success.

---

[9] See Appendix One.

Completion of an eighteen-year tour

Miss Hornby proceeded to Kampala and left Uganda for her long-overdue "furlough" in England. It can be construed from the dates given that she travelled home by air for the first time. In which case, she would have landed at several airports en route in Sudan, Egypt and Libya because the aeroplanes of that time could not fly all the way from Entebbe to London direct but had to stop and refuel. However, she does not mention the journey in her letter to supporters written in July 1954: *"If the one who wrote Psalm 42 had lived in England during June and July this year, don't you think he'd have written, 'As the hart panteth for the sunshine...'? I do. I long for the sun. The other day when I was in the train, the sun came out, and I said, 'Look! The sun!' Folks in the carriage looked at me and thought I was just simple. But it was a wonderful thing to see the sun in England!"* Obviously she had retained her sense of humour even during a wet English summer. She went on, *"I'm in England now, but every bit of me longs to be in Kigezi. I'd like to spend three or four years in the villages with the women and girls who have left school, and not be tied to any school. I'd take the girls' church-schools in my stride but as a 'side-show'. It is the district outside Kabale which needs help. At Kabale they've got Mrs Gregory-Smith and Mrs Balaba and others – they're all right . . . I'd like to meet as many G.F.S. members and other friends as I can . . . I feel I owe it to you to see you as I've been so long in Kigezi this tour (eighteen years). We need much prayer."* (5th July, 1954)

When she wrote this letter, she was staying in a house on the Sheen Road in Richmond, Surrey, close to where she was born seventy years before.[10] The King's Farm was no more and the land had been partly built-over with new houses. She may have attended services in Holy Trinity Church where she was baptized as an infant in 1884. The bomb damage caused by the recent War would have shocked her. Remarkably, her childhood home in Twickenham was not flattened along with many other buildings. People were rebuilding their lives and there was a spirit of optimism in the country. She no longer had close family relatives in England and her heart was amongst her people in Uganda. She retired officially on 31st October, 1954 and went back to live there, at the request of the Church.

---

[10] See photo on the next page.

Development of Hornby High School

Miss Hornby returned to her work as Schools Supervisor, based in Kabale and travelling around the District keeping watch over staffing, standards and finances in the Church schools which were grant-aided by the Government. She handed over this work in 1956. Therefore, she was on the spot to observe major up-grading of the school she founded in 1923. It was doing well and was selected by the Government to have a Junior Secondary School added to the six-year Primary Course. It became the first Junior Secondary Girls' School in the District. There were three missionaries on the staff, Miss Clayton heading the Primary Boarding School, Miss Clarke in charge of the one-year Teaching Course and Miss Betty Bromilow over the Junior Secondary class of twelve girls. Running one school with three strong-minded leaders must have been complicated at times but Miss Bromilow explained in a letter how their faith in Christ bound them together as a team, *"We know we need grace and broken-ness from the Lord as we work together as a team. Already we praise for the way in which He has dealt with us and helped us in various problems, showing again and again the need to bring our plans and problems to Him, to be cleansed of ourselves, and to be given completely to Him."* (19th February, 1955)

During 1955, new buildings for the two-year Junior Secondary School were constructed with Government funding, a grant of £22,000 allocated

KING'S FARM AVENUE, RICHMOND. *[PHOTO: E. TRAILL 2006]*

for the complete school. It was decided to relocate the girls' school at the far end of the mission station, beyond Kigezi High School for boys. The new straight road to it was dubbed "the Mile". As Miss Hornby had insisted from the beginning, it was important to keep the boys and girls apart especially in their teenage years, but a mere mile was no obstacle for young legs. The new Girls' School had to be fenced and well-guarded. Miss Bromilow was joined by Miss Margaret Burt from England and Mrs Irene Bisamunyu.[11] The latter was described by Miss Bromilow as *"a very capable and gifted African."* (13th October, 1956)

The new School was officially opened by Dr Joe Church on 6th October, 1956 in the presence of local Government officials, church leaders, parents and friends. It is likely that Miss Hornby was present. The school had been founded through prayer in 1923 and at this juncture another call for prayer was sent out, *"The message at the opening was: 'Except the Lord build the house, they labour in vain that build it.' Will you pray that the Lord may be the unseen Guest of our school – that the work-people will see Him in us, and that our visitors and those who come daily to sell us food may see Him, and that the girls will not only see Him but will want to walk with Him. These girls will be the wives of the future leaders of Kigezi and so this work is very important. Some of these girls have been walking with the Lord but they have found the old life very strong, and they need to see Jesus and His way. We praise Him for all He is doing for us, and I praise Him for His love and care of me in spite of my sometimes unbroken spirit."* (Betty Bromilow, 13th October, 1956)

A report at the end of 1956 said, *"Since moving in, much work has been done making approach roads and paths, and laying out the compound and games field. It has been a year with many difficulties and Satan clearly recognises the great spiritual possibilities of this school among the girls of Kigezi."* (T. Gregory-Smith, January 1957) Miss Hornby's legacy was expanding before her eyes. The school as an institution was an aspect of the "holistic mission" of the Church as it was understood at that

---

[11] See reference in Chapter Six to Irene Rosemary, daughter of the evangelist Andereya Nduluma. After her Primary education at Kabale Girls' School she was sent by Miss Clarke to Gayaza High School for secondary education. She completed a Course for Secondary School teaching and married Mr. E. Nathan Bisamunyu, the historian who later became Member of Parliament for Ndorwa, Kabale, under the Obote Government. (Source: Edward Bisamunyu, family papers).

time.[12] The standards of the school were high, both academically and in character-building. The aim was to give every girl the opportunity to achieve her best within the context of a disciplined community life. The possibility and outcomes of a living relationship with Jesus Christ as Saviour and Lord were explored but not forced upon the girls. In future years, committed Christian women educated at this school would become leaders in society as Uganda moved towards Independence in 1962.

To carry the story of the school forward, in 1961 it was renamed Hornby High School after its founder. By then, the Primary Section had moved along the Mile. This move left space on Rugarama Hill for Kigezi High School to expand on the boys' side. A Braille class was opened in 1969 for blind and partially sighted children. Much later, in 1981, the school was upgraded to Senior Secondary level, an "A" Level section was added and it continues to be a large, highly respected girls' school today. Miss Hornby's motto, "Mukundane" ("Love one another") remains in place, included in the school coat of arms.

[PHOTO: E. TRAILL 2010]

---

[12] Mission was seen as tripartite, Hospital-School-Church, ministering to body, mind and spirit in the local community. A "three-legged stool" was often used as an illustration. Mission would be unbalanced if one part was missing. See Matthew 4 v. 23 and 9 v. 35 and 3 John 2.

Handing on the baton

Miss Hornby was engaged in a relay race, constantly taking up responsibilities, running with them and then handing them on to other hands. The work of the Supervisor of the Church schools was growing apace. Rev. T. Gregory-Smith, affectionately known as "Greg", had been away during the War and returned to Kabale with his wife Irene in 1952. He was appointed as Schools' Supervisor, also the Chaplain to the Europeans. He surveyed and laid out the roads and drains on Rugarama Hill in his spare time. He held a degree in Engineering and so his hobby was to channel massive amounts of rainwater in appropriate ways. He was nicknamed the "Drain Brain" and his practical work endures to the present day. It must have been a relief to Miss Hornby to hand over the administrative side of the Schools' work to Greg and then continue with the visiting which she enjoyed. Together they supported the efforts of parents in the villages in their struggle to build schools, find teachers and set up the system in the way prescribed by the Government. He wrote in 1953, *"We now have thirty-nine schools with qualified teachers whose salaries we receive from the Government. The administration of this growing work becomes more formidable every year and we have reached the stage when the missionary has been spending nearly all his time and energies in the education office . . . The direction in which the country goes chiefly depends upon what sort of young men and women the schools produce, and that in turn depends to an overwhelming degree upon masters and mistresses. They vary greatly. Some are keen Christians amongst whom are numbered real spiritual leaders of the church. Others are indifferent and a few are actually antagonistic to the things of God, though they are classed as Christian workers. But what they are today, the country will be tomorrow. They hold the key."*

The population of Kigezi was growing rapidly, 480,000 in 1953, and some resettlement was taking place to sparsely populated areas. By the end of 1953, there were 200 Anglican Church schools in the District, of which 42 had reached the standard for Government funding. There were encouragements, *"At one place where there are boys' and girls' schools, over 100 children were saved within a few weeks. There had been no special meetings and previously there was only one saved master and one saved boy; it was a spontaneous work of the Holy Spirit. A wave of conviction and repentance swept through both schools. Piles of stolen property were returned to the teachers. Punishments ceased to be necessary. One boy had stolen some school keys and had used them for raiding local lock-up shops . . . It is our prayerlessness that makes Satan's task easy."* (T. Gregory-Smith, 1953 Report)

There were 550 village churches in Kigezi and the practice of holding "teranas" or weekend conventions was common. Teams of Christians from nearby churches would walk over the hills to another centre and spend Saturday and Sunday out of doors following a Bible theme chalked on a blackboard. It was always orderly with talks, testimonies and much singing and rejoicing. Miss Hornby and Miss Clarke enjoyed going to the teranas and taking brethren in their car. The news of the Gospel was proclaimed all over the District in this way. Great was the blessing.

In 1956 Miss Hornby finally handed over her part of the schools' work. Miss Clarke became responsible first for the girls' primary schools in the villages and then for all the schools when Greg went on leave. He came back to a wider appointment, to be the Educational Secretary of the Anglican Church in Ankole and Kigezi. The grant-aided schools in Kigezi alone now numbered over 50 and the work was too much for one person. Greg wrote as he moved on, *"On my last two-day safari I disposed of nearly £2,000 in cash as salaries to teachers in 18 schools. It is very difficult coping with all these wider responsibilities and still to be 'missionary in charge' of this station."* (Report, 1957)

The right time for bringing in a mature Ugandan teacher had come. They prayed and decided to write to Festo Kivengere in Tanganyika and offer him the post of Assistant Schools' Supervisor. As told in Coomes' biography, he and Merab heard God's calling to leave the Alliance Secondary School after 13 years' service but first he was asked by Bishop Stanway to go to Australia with Yohana Omari, new Assistant Bishop of Dodoma, as translator. The original six month visit was extended when Festo was invited to lead a mission amongst the Aborigines and in the Solomon Islands. Meanwhile, Merab and the girls settled into a three-roomed house at Kabale Girls' School where she became the Matron and the girls were enrolled in the school. At last in January 1960 Festo joined Miss Clarke in the Education office of the church at Kabale. They discussed their roles and agreed that Festo would oversee the teachers themselves and Miss Clarke would support the standards of teaching. This arrangement worked happily and both felt fulfilled in the work. As the date for Uganda's Independence approached, they decided with Christian grace that Miss Clarke should be the Assistant to Festo as Schools Supervisor. The schools work grew.

Then Festo felt the call to full-time evangelism and resigned at the end of 1961 and his friend James Katarikaawe took his place. Merab continued to be the Matron of Hornby High School. Festo embarked on a fruitful international ministry, then, in 1964, entered Pittsburgh Seminary for theological training. When he finished his studies, at Archbishop of Uganda, Leslie Brown's request, he was ordained Deacon on 11th June, 1966 in the Diocese of Pittsburgh. Later, he was ordained Priest by Bishop Dick Lyth in Kabale on December 10th, 1967. All this pleased Miss Hornby very much.

Retirement in Kinkiizi

Miss Hornby, although young in heart, gratefully accepted the offer of a plot of land near Nyakatare in Kinkiizi County, down in the lush Rift Valley, where she could build a small house for her retirement years. Apparently it had two rooms, a bedroom and a large sitting-room, with an outside African-style kitchen, wash place and store. She employed a house-girl and a gardener who grew some of their food. She loved flowers and cultivated a colourful garden in front of the house, with roses around the door. Mrs Betty Thomson (nee Bromilow) remembers, *"It was a real cottage garden, but she grew her own vegetables. She had very basic furniture, made locally out of packing cases and an iron framed bed (a luxury)."* (Questionnaire, August 2010) She had a simple diet and lived contentedly, fitting in with the people and supporting the local church. She used to tell her Old Girls and elders of Kigezi, *"I like the Bakiga; the Bakiga are very hard working and very kind to me; they help me in everything and treat me like a queen . . . I don't intend to leave Kigezi. I will die here and my people will bury me."* (Quoted from "History of Hornby High School" booklet pub. 1997)

Miss Hornby maintained her car and occasionally visited Kabale. Stories about her exploits were told affectionately. One day she rolled into Kabale with only a drop of petrol in her tank, the car taking its last gasp at the "Esso" Petrol Station, the first in the town. She said she ran her car mostly on prayer. Sheelagh Warren, newly arrived as a teacher at Gayaza High School, will never forget her experience with Miss Hornby, *"I vividly recall that we drove all round Lake Bunyonyi – her wish – to greet all and sundry. She drove, but didn't like going alone. I took her a cabbage/cauliflower because no vegetables would grow in her garden. She was greeted rapturously at every stop by young and old. She had a note saying 'BREAK' on her car and I thought it meant 'BRAKE' at the time. She was very humble and matter of fact. Her home was very simple. She told me they gave her the plot because nothing would grow there. She visited people in need all the time."* (27th July, 2002)

Within her first year in Kinkiizi she had a visit from Professor Harold Ingrams of Makerere University who was writing a book on Uganda prior to Independence. He devoted several pages to Miss Hornby, showing how much he valued her story. He enjoyed the journey from Kabale. *"We started for Kinkiizi County by climbing into the mountains through valleys whose sides were impressively covered with cultivation. It was a remarkable road, aligned and built by a Muganda, one Kiwanika, who was works supervisor of the Kigezi district council. We drove through a forest of pine and cypress. Mafuga forest is a creation of the forestry department: the cypress trees are natives of Mexico and the southern states of the U.S.A. The cottage of Miss Hornby at Kirima, just off the road but with miles and miles of impenetrable forest all round, stands in a perfect sunlit glade. She calls it 'Advice', because everyone gave her so much advice on how to build it. It was not a year old, and had cost her 7,000 shillings."*

Harking back to her early years in Kigezi, Miss Hornby told him, *"The Government had strong objections to women travelling about the country alone. I took no notice of this and travelled with a man of the tribe. He carried a spear with him and when I was through the territory of one tribe, I would be met by a man of the next tribe, also with a spear. The man I had come with would stick his spear in the ground saying 'Muntu yeitu' – 'This is your person', and so I was handed on from tribe to tribe. I travelled so much in little known parts that the D.C. got agitated and wrote to the Government about it. Then I was given a Muganda soldier to protect me. He got very drunk on my first safari with him, so of course I had to appeal to the chief of the territory I was in to remove him. After that I had no more trouble and was allowed to travel wherever I liked."* They went on to talk about the planned cultivation on the hillsides and other signs of progress. *"She said she thought all that had been done was wonderful, but that we'd gone too fast. When Bishop Aberi Balya, the saintly African Bishop of Fort Portal, came down to Kigezi he said to them, 'I marvel at your civilization, but you go too fast. In Toro we have the mvule tree (one of the most beautiful trees in East Africa). It grows slowly but it never blows down in a storm. Down here in Kigezi your tree is the eucalyptus, which grows fast and blows over when the storm comes."* (Ingrams, 1960, p.213-218.) A party of chiefs and elders arrived and the conversation went on, touching on tribal customs and modern problems. Miss Hornby enjoyed having visitors and was a born conversationalist.

Miss Hornby did not write any more letters or reports for the Ruanda Mission magazine, and her correspondence with the Girls' Friendly Society had long finished. That organisation underwent great changes after the Second World War. It is now called "The Women's Platform" and focuses on gender issues.

Information about her retirement years in Kinkiizi is scanty. *Ruanda Notes* in early 1957 says *"Miss Hornby, although officially retired, continues to 'mother' the women and girls of Kinkiizi as she visits them from her home in Nyakatare. Recently she has been sending out 117 Scripture Union Notes in English to some of the educated young men and a few girls in Kigezi who can understand them. She asks prayer for these, and praise that they are wanted."* Margaret Oliver (nee Burt) visited her and told her news of Kabale Girls' Junior Secondary School, where she was the Headmistress. *"She always said, 'I had the best of it. You have so many rules.' Unlike Western society today she was content to live simply and trust the Lord. She showed her faith in God by her care for people around her and her sacrificial life."* (Questionnaire, July 2010)

Two clergymen with long memories helped in our research. Rev. Canon William Mbarubukeye remembered her walking with a stick in old age, also her visits when she was Schools' Supervisor during Christmas and Easter holidays when she and Miss Clarke would stay at the Kihiihi Rest House and go into the Queen Elizabeth National Park. He said that she concentrated on Bible reading and teaching, leading prayers and visiting people in need. When his own house was burnt down, she helped him. She also paid school fees for poor students. (Questionnaire 5th May, 2002.)

Rev. Daniel Kizimpeire of Bushere I, Kihiihi Church of Uganda, said that Miss Hornby shared the word of God with all who attended the Church and did a lot of visiting. She used to sing with the Christians and the students and, on occasion, she did preach. She believed strongly in God. Her faith led her to help people to build schools and churches, for example she gave furniture to Kihiihi Primary School and iron sheets to roof their big Church. She taught and helped the wives of Church leaders. (Questionnaire 8th June, 2002.)

Ten years went by, during which time Uganda achieved Independence on October 9th, 1962. Miss Hornby lived out her life behind the headlines, quietly and contentedly facing the challenges and opportunities of each day. She had a very close relationship with her Lord and Master and talked to Him about everything. Her wooden plaque RABBONI (my great Master) hung in her sitting room. Her books were her companions in her home. Presumably she had a radio so that she could hear some news from outside. She forgot about dates and birthdays, hence the confusion about her age when she returned to Kabale. Her long life of venturesome love had come full circle, now she was surrounded by love in an African village. But she could not stay there for ever.

Chapter Eight
1966 – 1972
A STORY-RICH LIFE

A period of rapid change in Uganda

Miss Hornby, now generally known as Kaaka Hornby, lived for ten years in warm, lush Kinkiizi County near the Game Park which formed the border with the Democratic Republic of Congo. It was about as far from the capital Kampala as one could be in Uganda and village life was totally absorbing. Many political upheavals were taking place but she was largely unaware of them. She was more concerned with her neighbours and their various needs, attending to births, marriages and deaths, rejoicing with those who rejoiced, and weeping with those who wept. One mature student at Bishop Barham University College said he was named "Bestone" because Miss Hornby held him as a baby and said, "He's the best one!"

It sounds an idyllic life, living simply in her little house, eating local food and home-made bread, spending time in Church and in Bible study and prayer, visiting neighbours and entertaining all who came to see her with many stories of past days. She maintained her spiritual discipline and focus on the Lord Jesus. In old age, rather like Amy Carmichael of Dohnavur, to whom reference was made in Chapter Five, or St Paul living a restricted life in Rome, she had passed from the phase of active fighting service to "The Keeping of the Charge".[1] She had an intimate experience of the presence and love of the Lord. However, she was ageing and becoming frail. Her eightieth birthday in 1964 passed without her realising it. She told us that she forgot about years and birthdays in Kinkiizi.

---

[1] This is a reference to the work of the Levites in Numbers 1 v. 53b: "The Levites shall keep charge of the tabernacle of the testimony." See Houghton p. 289 ff. for a description of Amy Carmichael's ministry late in life after thirty-six years in India without a break, working amongst women and girls. Such people give an example of godliness in years of retirement.

FIRST AFRICAN
ARCHBISHOP OF
UGANDA, RT.
REV. ERICA
SABIITI WITH
CANON JOHN
TAYLOR, GEN.
SEC. OF THE
C.M.S.
[PHOTO: E.
RUGUMAYO]

At Provincial level, the Church of Uganda in 1966 received the first African Archbishop in the person of Rev. Erica Sabiiti who succeeded Archbishop Leslie Brown when he retired. It was decided to divide the Diocese of Ankole-Kigezi into two and Rev. Dick Lyth, former Headmaster of Kigezi High School and now Christian Rural Service worker in Kigezi, was chosen to be the first Bishop of Kigezi. He spent most of 1966 preparing for this new role, bringing his experience and administrative gifts as a former District Commissioner in the Sudan to the task of setting up a new Diocese. His wife Nora was the daughter

AFTER THE CONSECRATION OF THE FIRST BISHOP OF KIGEZI
LEFT TO RIGHT:
DR AND MRS A. STANLEY SMITH (NORA'S PARENTS), BISHOP LYTH, MICHAEL,
MRS LYTH (DICK'S MOTHER), JENNY, MRS BALABA, SUE, BISHOP SHALITA OF ANKOLE,
MRS NORA LYTH

of Dr and Mrs Algie Stanley Smith and they had a young family. He carefully considered what would be best for Miss Hornby and proposed that she should come to live in Kabale again, closer to medical services and within the wider community which could give her the care and support she needed. Therefore, a small two-roomed house near the bend in the road going up Rugarama Hill was made available for her. It had an outside latrine, wash place and kitchen and a pretty garden on the hillside bright with flowers. Inside, we remember a comfortable sitting room with bookcases, the text "RABBONI" on the wall, dark wood furniture with cushions and a peaceful atmosphere. She had a bedroom behind and a sink with a single cold tap in the small corridor beside the back door. She saw the good sense in the move and settled quickly in her new home, assisted by her faithful house servant named Lilian.

What had happened in Kampala?[2]

When Uganda's Independence was declared on 9th October 1962, a coalition government was set up consisting of the Uganda Peoples' Congress allied with the Kabaka Yekka party of Buganda. The defeated Democratic Party formed the Opposition. The elected Prime Minister was Dr Milton Obote, leader of the U.P.C. The fine new Parliament building and offices nearby housed the government and the civil service. The Kabaka Yekka party soon left the coalition. The Ugandan army was largely composed of Northerners who had proved to be adept soldiers under the Protectorate administration. A tall man from the Kakwa people named Idi Amin was Deputy Commander of the army. He had received military training in England and was a heavyweight boxing champion.

To summarise the story, in 1965 the illicit theft of gold, ivory and coffee from the Congo came to the attention of Parliament. Dr Obote himself and General Idi Amin were under accusation, but the case was never proved and instead the accusers were detained. In February 1966, Dr Obote suspended the Independence Constitution and assumed dictatorial powers. He made General Idi Amin the Army Chief of Staff. They feared that Buganda would secede and therefore they carried out an attack on the Kabaka's Palace, forcing the Kabaka himself to go into exile in England, where he died three years later. Buganda District was

---

[2]   Political background here based on account in (later President) Museveni, Yoweri Kaguta: *Sowing the Mustard Seed*, Chapter Four, 1997.

declared to be in a state of emergency, which made it necessary to seek official permission to travel across the district boundary. Dr Obote claimed that he was overthrowing feudalism and therefore he forged friendships with socialist regimes elsewhere, like China and the U.S.S.R. "The Move to the Left" was a slogan of the times. He introduced "The Common Man's Charter." Uganda was declared a Republic, a one-party state, with Dr Obote as the President. The traditional monarchies including the Rutakirwa John Bikangaga, elected leader of Kigezi, were kept under control. It is interesting to note that his wife Grace, the *Nyinaboona* ("mother of all"), was one of Miss Hornby's original Old Girls, a gracious Christian lady. The Member of Parliament for Kabale was none other than Mr Nathan Bisamunyu, mentioned several times before. His wife Irene was another of Miss Hornby's girls, a vivacious person who enjoyed her public duties and shared her Christian faith.

VISIT OF PRESIDENT MILTON OBOTE TO ST PETER'S CATHEDRAL, APRIL 9TH 1967.
LEFT TO RIGHT: *[PHOTO: MR EZRA RWENDEIRE]*
RT REV. RICHARD LYTH, BISHOP OF KIGEZI; H.E. DR MILTON OBOTE, PRESIDENT OF UGANDA; MRS GRACE BIKANGAGA, NYINABOONA OF KIGEZI; H.E. JOHN BIKANGAGA, RUTAKIRWA OF KIGEZI; MR MPAMBARA, SECRETARY GENERAL OF KIGEZI.

In April 1967, President Obote and his entourage arrived in Kabale for an official visit. The town was gaily decorated. According to the printed programme which had been distributed, he arrived one and a half days late and gave a speech in the Stadium. Then he was entertained to an official Reception followed by a Ball at the White Horse Inn. On Sunday morning, April 9th, he attended the 10.00 a.m. Service in St Peter's Cathedral, Rugarama. Miss Hornby would have heard the drone of the traffic moving up and down the hill and may have attended the Service. Everything was on time. Bishop Lyth preached an excellent sermon based on the story of the crossing of the Red Sea, with enemies to be faced like Disease, Poverty, Ignorance and Hatred between tribes and in the home. It was a challenge to all present.

A little haven on Rugarama Hill

Distances in Africa are so great that happenings far away can have little effect locally. Miss Hornby quickly caught up with the changes occurring in Kabale. The Town was growing with a strong and prosperous community of Asian traders who were building and operating shops and businesses large and small. She made good

KABALE MAIN STREET IN THE 1960s. *[PHOTO: ROGER F.L. WILKINS]*

friends with some of these people. The Government Hospital had several expatriate doctors and nurses. The two secondary schools, Kigezi High School and Kigezi College, Butobere, were expanding and had a number of teachers recruited under the British Government aid scheme. Hornby High School and Kabale Preparatory School (K.P.S.) were growing and had several missionaries on the staff. Amongst the growing community of expatriates in Kabale were Christians who appreciated an English Service. Kabale had a golf course, a club and a good hotel, the White Horse Inn. The tourist trade was beginning.

VIEW OVER KABALE IN THE 1960s. *[PHOTO: ROGER F.L. WILKINS]*

Miss Hornby's little home became a haven where young and old could go for quiet visits after the heat and activity of the day. Mrs. Doreen Sharp lived with her family in the old mission house next door and recalled, *"Many people used to visit her to talk and get advice about their work. I was going out from Kabale to take Sunday School courses for teachers and pastors in rural churches. When I returned, she was a 'haven' to go and see and talk over any problems. I always felt refreshed and renewed after being with her."* (Questionnaire, 2002)

Sometimes the tall figure of Miss Nan Read, Headmistress of K.P.S., would climb up the path to her door. She remembered *"She prayed about everything and freely talked of Him and trusted Him. She was a pioneer who* said 'keep at it' and tackled difficult things. She advised me not to worry about lost keys etc." (Questionnaire, 27th July 2002)

Miss Jean Hurford, on the teaching staff of K.P.S., remembered: "She loved having visitors in her latter days when she was less mobile and her sight was failing. I used to go after school when possible to read her Bible to her. She knew exactly where the passage was to read. She gave good advice (albeit sometimes impractical for modern days of structured education and curricula.) She would be very firm with wrongdoers, pointing out what God says, and the outcome. She was an extraordinary pioneer belonging to the early days of Uganda. She had great vision in starting girls' education, 'Educate a girl, educate a family,' especially as regards Christian upbringing. She suffered much deprivation of life style without grumbling because God enabled and envisioned her. She battled through many setbacks, loneliness and difficulties, proving His power to work to establish His kingdom." (Questionnaire, 3rd September 2002)

After Doreen Sharp and her family left Kabale, a German family, Rev. Reinhold and Elisabeth Abraham with their two young children, arrived to live in the big old mission house next to Miss Hornby's little home. She became a special family friend and Elisabeth recorded some homely details, "Kaaka Hornby was one of the unique characters of the early days! I first met her in 1970 when she was already old. My memories are not very spiritual, although I remember her as a really spiritual person. When we lived next to her, we used to ask her if she wanted us to do some shopping for her. Then she would ask us to bring her 'a litre of butter and a metre of milk – or whatever these new names are.' When we had bought her things she would say, 'There is a hundred shilling note in Romans Eight!' When we opened her Bible, the money was there! I was deeply moved by her clear and simple life right to the end." (Letter, 22nd May, 2002)

Visitors came from further afield. Betty Bromilow had married Professor David Thomson and they lived in Kampala. She recalls, "Miss Hornby loved children and my four still remember her. We used to visit Kabale often from Makerere University. The children would give her flowers and visit her little house. My memory is of a great personality with a sense of fun, sure of God's presence with her, loving people. She loved her Bible. Her prayers were very definite, practical and direct to God. She had a clear concept of the Fatherhood of God. She loved the hymn 'Dear Lord and Father of mankind, forgive our foolish ways.' I smile when I remember her and praise the Lord for her commitment to further God's kingdom in Uganda, especially Kigezi."(Questionnaire, August 10th 2010)

As mentioned in the Introduction, one day, the District Medical Officer, Dr Dick Vinden called to see her and look into her papers because he was the local representative of the British High Commission in Uganda. It was important when the political situation was unstable for everyone to have their documents in order. He checked her passport and noted that she was born on October 4th, 1884, a fact which has been proved again in our research. This took her by surprise because she had told many people that she was born in 1886! This mistake is still being perpetuated. As friends at the time, we were amused and added two years to the number of her next birthday. We found out that she enjoyed home-made jam and it made an ideal present.

LETTER FROM MISS HORNBY TO MADGE QUINN, 1969.
[REPRODUCED WITH PERMISSION]

Boosting the morale of young teachers

From her vantage point, Miss Hornby saw numerous vehicles of all sizes toiling up Rugarama Hill and a constant stream of young and older people on foot. Kigezi High School, further up the hill, was the destination of much of the traffic. It was upgraded in 1965 to Senior Secondary level when about 60 students were enrolled including a small number of girls. The capacity increased every year through a continuous building programme funded by the Uganda Government and the World Bank. By 1972, there were 600 students on the roll, including 120 girls and 25 members of teaching staff. The headmasters in this period were Mr Zebuloni Kabaza (1965-69) and Mr John Martin (1969 onwards), with Mr Dudley Carr serving as Acting Headmaster in the interregnum. An observation in the 1972 Golden Jubilee magazine of the school hints at the pressures endured during these years: *"Inevitably we have come face to face with all the inherent challenges of rapid development . . . When this occurs, the present tends to absorb all the energy at the expense of the future, and the future becomes unpredictable, and when it places its own challenges, they find everybody unprepared."*

The teaching staff became fairly balanced between Ugandans and expatriates who worked together and shared the many responsibilities within boarding school life. Teaching their lessons was perhaps the easiest part of their work. They also had to oversee the health and welfare of the students in their dormitories, keep discipline, ensure the food in the dining room was sufficient, organise sports and games, supervise the Library, work out the timetable for lessons, provide weekend entertainment and take turns to lead and speak at Assemblies and Chapel Services. Clubs and societies flourished, including Scripture Union. Decisions were made at lengthy staff meetings which sought consensus. Diaries from the time reveal the multitude of activities which kept the teachers occupied all day, every day, in term-time. It was life "in the fast lane" or "24/7" before those phrases became common parlance in the 1990s. There were many crises and difficulties. Sometimes, cultural differences emerged which needed to be explored. The young people we were teaching ranged in age from 12 to 25 years, or occasionally even older because of the difficulties village people faced in sending their children to Primary School. The students felt under pressure from other members of their families who saw them as the salaried providers of the future. Sometimes the pressures in their minds erupted in a tense, rebellious attitude which bound them in solidarity with one another. Others found solace in escaping under cover of darkness to local bars and returned drunk.

There was a full-scale riot in July 1969 when the boys of Senior One and Two stoned the dining hall where the first-ever school dance was in progress as a protest at being excluded, although they were provided with an outdoor film show in compensation! The next day, the whole school was sent home. In July 1968 there were days of tension in Kigezi High School when it was difficult to teach, but a strike was averted by prayer and diplomacy. In December 1968, there was a riot over food served in the dining hall. We lived "from crisis to crisis", as Miss Foibe Biteete our colleague observed. Miss Hornby kept a prayerful watch on the situation.

It was refreshing for some of the teachers to go and consult Miss Hornby. One time, she showed us a small piece of rock which had been skilfully covered in decorative beading by a school girl. There was a hole where a thread had broken, revealing the rock underneath. *"See this,"* she said, *"Civilisation is just a veneer, very thin. Every so often, the real Africa pops up."*

Madge Quinn recalls, *"She walked with a stick. She seemed small and thin and had white hair in a loose bun. She talked in a decisive way, not at all vague. She spoke quietly and listened well. She said, 'My child, I'm glad I'm not in your position. Things were far easier in my day.' Early in 1971 we had a 'flu' epidemic and she came up to the School to encourage us. She visited the Library which had been turned into a Sick Bay with Mr Tim Oakley in charge as Health Master. She told us lovely stories about the early days when things were really tough. She had a ministry of encouragement to younger people. Amongst her many good friends were several Asians. We were glad that she died early in 1972 before the awful events of that year, when all the Asians were forcibly expelled."* (Questionnaire, 23rd June 2002)

On September 3rd, 1967, Miss Madge Quinn and her housemate, the author, were returning from Kampala in their Volkswagen 'Beetle' car. It broke down on the valley road a few miles after Muhanga, a lonely place, and they were stranded for the night. They were escorted on foot back to Muhanga by some friendly village boys who put them into the care of a Christian family who had a shop. They spent the night safely in the grain store at the rear of the building, with rats and fleas for company, and returned to Kabale by bus the next morning. There were no telephones and so the friends in Kabale were very anxious. When she heard the story, Miss Hornby came round to see us and prayed fervently with thanksgiving that, *"these two of Your children who were lost in the heart of Africa have been found and are safe and well."* We felt very fond of Miss Hornby and grateful for her care and concern for us.

A romance developed between two of the teachers, Tim Oakley and Barbara Thorne, in 1970. Miss Hornby invited them to tea several times and after they became engaged early in 1971 she said to them, *"I think that the Lord is going to return soon but I hope it's not too soon otherwise you two won't have very long to enjoy a married life."* (Barbara Oakley, August 21st 2010) They have treasured this saying ever since.

The lighter side of life

Tensions and crises were only part of the story. As a community we had many laughs, hilarious times and much encouragement in our work and witness for Christ. Coping with the local language Rukiga was one important aspect. The author was appointed Health Mistress at her first staff meeting in January 1967 on the basis of holding a Girl Guide Camp First Aid Certificate, which made her more qualified than any other member of the teaching staff. In support, one of the nurses from Kabale Hospital visited the school every morning. The Health Teacher had a wobbly wooden cupboard in the Science Room with three basic medicines. Two large brown bottles were labelled "Magnesium Trisilicate" and "Kaolin Mixture". A green squeezy bottle contained "Cough Mixture". These were appropriately labelled by the outgoing Health Mistress, Lucy Wilkins (U.S. Peace Corps): "Above the belt", "Below the belt" and "One squirt down each needy gullet". A smaller bottle labelled "Tinc. Benz. Co." was apparently for application to wounds. There was also a supply of cotton wool and sticking plaster, Dettol antiseptic, an enamel bowl and a jerry can of water. There were no rubber gloves, which would be essential today due to the threat of Aids. The "Dispensary" opened daily at 4 p.m. after classes. One day, after the students had gone, two cooks came from the School Kitchen. One had a wound on his arm, the other a wound on his leg. They did not speak English and the Health Mistress was alone. She had only spent a month in Kigezi. It was necessary to ask the men to sit down. A moment's thought produced a Rukiga word, *"Tushabe"*, which Canon Zaribugire used to say in Church, after which everyone sat down. (It really meant, "Let us pray.") At this, the men smiled, knelt down, closed their eyes and held their hands in an attitude of prayer. She did not even know the Lord's Prayer by heart and struggled to contain her amusement. Somehow, the necessary First Aid was administered and the cooks returned to their work. Gales of laughter were heard around the Hill! Miss Hornby with her lively sense of humour was very amused. The author gained the nickname "Tushabe", whispered by girls in the dormitories when she came with a torch at "lights out" time.

Scripture Union and the Sharp's Island Weekend May 1967

The Scripture Union had branches at Kigezi High School and Kigezi College, Butobere. A joint weekend Conference was arranged with the theme of "Growth" to take place on Sharp's Island, Lake Bunyonyi, using the old house which had been unoccupied since Dr Len and Mrs

SCRIPTURE UNION CONFERENCE ON SHARP'S ISLAND, MAY 1967.
[PHOTO: M. QUINN]

Esther Sharp left in 1961.[3] We travelled there in an old boat called *The African Queen* which chugged across the calm waters of the lake. There were only six girls amongst more than 40 students. Part of the aim was to do gardening and maintenance work on the house, then to live, cook and eat together with sessions studying God's Word.[4] Mr Albert Taylor from S.U. Headquarters in Kampala was the main speaker. On the Sunday morning we went in huge iron boats with paddles to attend the Church Service on Bwama Island and to visit the Leprosy Hospital and Settlement. Miss Hornby was staying there, visiting Sister Pat Gilmer who was the new Leprosy Control Officer for Kigezi. It was Pentecost Sunday and Albert Taylor preached on the fruit of the Spirit. After the Service, we went around the Hospital and heard many testimonies from patients, especially one disfigured old lady named Mary whose joy in the Lord and simple words convicted many of the students, especially one named David Komunda.[5] He received Christ as his Saviour and Lord that day and went on to serve Him faithfully in hospital work.

Mr Dudley Carr who was a leader of the Conference wrote, *"I have a clear recollection of sensing that the supernatural presence of the Holy Spirit was moving amongst the students that weekend. Although I did not witness it for myself, I was told of what seems to have been a spontaneous outbreak of dancing and singing and rejoicing in the Lord amongst some of those present. As a general comment, as I have said to many folk since leaving Uganda, the role of Scripture Union in adding to and building up the Church was absolutely pivotal. Almost every Ugandan I have met seems to have a testimony about the impact of Scripture Union school groups, Conferences or missions upon their lives."* (Letter, 23rd August, 2010)

---

[3] Dr and Mrs. Sharp retired to Mombasa to live at a low altitude near the Indian Ocean, for health reasons. See Makower (2008) "Not a Gap Year but a Lifetime" p. 241-246.

[4] Notes for one of the Bible Studies on the theme "The struggle for survival" began: "A plant faces many dangers before it grows to maturity . . . but poor conditions can cause plants to become durable and tough. In the same way, difficulties and temptations can be of real value to us. While Satan tempts us that we may fall, God tests us so that we may stand and grow." References included Luke 4 vv. 1-14 and I Cor. 10 v. 13.

[5] David Komunda became Dispenser at Mengo Hospital, Kampala, and has served there faithfully as Hospital Manager for many years up to the present time.

The Blood-brotherhood Ceremony at Kabale, January 1st 1968

Miss Hornby and Dr Algie Stanley Smith received great honour from the people of Kigezi in recognition of their services. He wrote at length about the Ceremony, published in a church newspaper. Here is a summary of the article: *"On January 1st this year the District Council of Kigezi arranged a celebration in honour of the foundation of the Republic of Uganda. They decided to invite a certain number of people, foreigners to Kigezi, who they felt had served the country. Six were chosen, a Lango from the North, a Doctor from Busoga, who had been much beloved while in Kigezi, a Muganda, and three missionaries, one a Roman Catholic Priest, and the other two Protestants, Miss Constance Hornby and myself. All were to receive blood-brotherhood . . . The ceremony was held out on an open hillside in a natural amphitheatre, just as it would have been in the old days . . . There was a high table on which were placed two simple African stools . . . The Secretary-General of Kigezi as titular head of the District stood before the people and recited the deeds and services of each one in turn . . . Then the Master of Ceremonies called out in a loud voice to all the people, 'Is there any reason why this man/ woman should not be admitted to our blood-brotherhood?' And all the people answered 'No!' Then the Secretary General mounted the table and sat on the stool and each followed and sat on the opposite one. As we held hands high up for all to see, an oath of mutual loyalty was exchanged and a new name given to each one. We were each given a robe, a spear and a bill hook . . . Dear old Miss Hornby was named Kaaka (Grandmother), for she has been a true 'Mother' to the women and girls of Kigezi . . . She is a frail old lady now, but she entered into it all with the zest of perpetual youth, and at the end she said a few words of thanks, most of all eager that in all this recital of men's deeds the real glory should go to the Master under whose orders she had come and served for forty-five years right there among the people."*

In commenting on the ceremony, Dr Algie added, *"What a remarkable thing it is that this custom of 'Omukago' was so widely practised among the nations, a sign that the partaking of blood ends the enmity between man and man, and between clan and clan; and this is surely a God-given parable of the 'precious blood of Christ', the only means by which we can be reconciled to God, and thereby be admitted into that Blood-brotherhood in our Lord which is now uniting people of every tribe and culture in the world."*[6]

---

[6] Extract from the article by Dr A. Stanley Smith in the English Churchman, February 16th, 1968.

After the ceremony, according to Miss Jean Hurford, Miss Hornby did not talk about it because she felt it was a secret. (Questionnaire, 3rd September 2002) The above account by Dr Algie shows that there was nothing unpleasant in the ceremony, all was in the open. Miss Margaret Walker, nursing sister at Kisiizi Hospital, remembers, *"She was pleased to be made a 'blood brother'. She gave Judy Ingle the beaded stick and special costume presented to her on that occasion."*(Questionnaire, 6th September 2002)

Concern for children with Special Needs

In these years, Miss Hornby became aware of the many children in Kigezi who could not join the ordinary schools because of some physical challenge. She heard about the special training school for teachers of the blind at Iganga in Busoga, where she herself had worked more than fifty years before. She talked to a young friend, a

HORNBY HIGH SCHOOL SECONDARY: THE BLIND SECTION IN 2010.
[PHOTO: E. TRAILL]

Ugandan teacher named David Tindyebwa who was at that time working in a Moslem school and persuaded him to transfer to the schools founded by the C.M.S. and to train as a Braille teacher. He went to Iganga and completed the course under two C.M.S. missionaries, Miss Nancy Britten and Miss Pat Holder. Because of his connection with Miss Hornby, he was enabled to go to Thika in Kenya for further training. He came back to his home area and joined the staff of Hornby High School with the task of setting up the section for blind children. He started with three boys and three girls, selected fairly from the six counties of Kigezi. Miss Lilian Clarke paid great attention to this new class and doubtless told

MR DAVID TINDYEBWA, TUTOR, SITTING ON MISS HORNBY'S CHAIR WORKING ON BRAILLE TYPEWRITER.
[PHOTO: E. TRAILL]

Miss Hornby all about the progress of the pupils. How proud they would be today of one of the first pupils, a boy named Benon Ndaziboneye from Kisoro in Bufumbira County, who holds a Master's degree and works as a Rehabilitation Officer in Kampala! He is married to a Nurse and they have sighted children.

Amin's Regime begins January 1971

Kigezi seemed like a little world on its own where life progressed with some degree of order and normality. In the capital, a power struggle between Dr Milton Obote and his Army Chief of Staff, General Idi Amin, was raging. It culminated early in 1971 when the President was in Singapore for the Commonwealth Leaders' Conference. On January 25th a military coup took place, which took many people by surprise. The new Government was popular and there was dancing in the streets of Kampala as the years of mismanagement and corruption under Dr Milton Obote came to an end. A professional teacher, Mr Edward Rugumayo, became the Minister of Education, and a doctor was chosen as the Minister of Health. There was general euphoria and the sense of a new beginning, which lasted for a few months. President Amin himself visited Kabale and opened the new buildings at Kigezi High School on May 1st, 1971.[7]

SAMPLE OF BANK NOTE UNDER PRESIDENT AMIN

---

[7] David Komunda was by now the Head Prefect and made a speech of loyalty, concluding, "I wish to assure you that Kigezi High School students are ready to work day and night for the progress of this country, taking the right channels for the benefit of our citizens. Hence we feel duty bound to fulfil our School Motto 'I Serve' and our National Motto 'For God and My Country'. Thank you very much." (Speech to the President of Uganda, 1st May 1971)

MISS HORNBY OUTSIDE HER SMALL HOUSE
ON RUGARAMA HILL, 1970.
[PHOTO: E. RWENDEIRE]

Miss Hornby would have observed the Presidential convoy going up and down Rugarama Hill, this time with a preponderance of smartly dressed military personnel. Later, things took an ominous turn and the country entered a very dark time, as is well known and documented. The light of Christ burned brightly and the Church actually grew during the time of persecution. As stated before, Miss Hornby was spared the worst of the suffering which happened after her death.

Waiting to be called Home

Miss Hornby became increasingly frail. Her eyesight was failing and she struggled to walk up the Hill with her stick. She attended the tea party which Bishop and Mrs Lyth gave for school teachers in February 1970. It can be seen from this photograph that she had little physical strength. She kept going courageously and continued to walk slowly around the Hill. On March 30th, 1970 she had a fall and was brought to our house for First Aid. Later, she fell again and was taken to Mengo Hospital with a broken arm on June 10th. She wore a sling afterwards for some time and came back to Kabale to resume her normal life. She began to feel ready for her Lord and Master to call her to her home in Heaven. She used to sit on her veranda in the sunshine watching the passing traffic and enjoying the fresh air, the birdsong and the bright flowers. She felt at peace. She said to her friends, *"You know I love to go out and sit on my chair in the sunshine on the veranda ready for Him, to meet Him when He comes to call me."* (Nora Lyth, letter August 2002)

One of our last memories of her was just before Christmas 1971 when a group of teachers went to sing carols to her on a dark, starlit night. In the light of a hurricane lantern, she came to her door clad in a red fluffy cardigan over her white flannelette nightgown. Her snow white hair framed her face and her blue eyes shone with joy. It was a picture to remember.

On 26th December 1971, a short Holy Communion Service was held in Miss Hornby's home. Bishop Dick and Nora Lyth were there, and her father, Dr Algie Stanley Smith gave the address, speaking simply and movingly, *"I think it is wonderfully fitting to take part in a communion service at Christmas time, to remember the birth and the death of our Lord Jesus – the cradle and the cross; and it is all the more precious to us gathered here in Miss Hornby's house, as if the Lord was inviting us to meet Him here in Africa in 1971. Let me read it to you . . . 'Then came the day of unleavened bread when the Passover lamb had to be sacrificed; so the disciples came to Jesus and said 'Where do you want us to prepare to eat the Passover?' and He said, 'I want you to go to the country of Kigezi, to the little white house of a dear old servant of mine they call Kaaka Hornby to join with her in this service of fellowship and remembrance. But don't make elaborate preparations; the preparation I want is the preparation of the heart. The purpose of this meal is to remind you of what God did for you, when He delivered you from bondage, and brought you into liberty. It is only a simple meal I want, so none will be excluded, just an ordinary loaf of bread, and some wine that the common folk are accustomed to . . . There is deep meaning in the choice of these two symbols. Bread, not grain, and wine, not grapes; grain must be crushed and ground and passed through fire. I will explain to you that I am to be the bread of life that gives life to the world . . . and I speak to you of the crushing of the grapes, for my lifeblood must be poured out . . . to cleanse you from all sin . . . I want you to keep on remembering with thanksgiving all that my body and my blood have done for you . . . Do you know why I particularly want you to go to that little white bungalow in Kigezi? It is because my dear old friend and servant who lives there, is so much longing for me to come and take her to Myself."*
(Dr Algie Stanley Smith, notes typed by Mrs Nora Lyth, August 2002)

How the end came

On Tuesday, 8th February, 1972, Bishop Lyth came to our house in the afternoon with excitement in his face, "Miss Hornby is going to glory!" The next day, we heard that she had passed away during the night. It is best to let Mrs Nora Lyth tell the story, in a letter written to Miss

Hornby's brother:[8] *"She's had a few ups and downs recently, but was not in bed except for the last day. On Monday night she started coughing, and her lungs began to get rather full up. We called the doctor to see her three times in the last few days, and I believe she was helped by the drugs which were given, though she resisted them in her usual way right up to the end! I was with her on and off through Tuesday, and spent the night with her. She was not in much pain at all, just tired with the effort of breathing, and her indomitable spirit showed in her insisting on getting up for tea on Tuesday! She was conscious though sleepy during the night, and frequently commented on verses and hymns that I read to her, and mentioned other people and their troubles. She also talked about you quite a bit and about your latest letter. She spoke about the Lord so often, 'Please take me, Lord Jesus', 'Jesus is all I want', 'He must be everything and I will be nothing'. At 3 a.m. she asked for a cup of tea, and drank it, then after five minutes she was with the Lord, quite peacefully . . . Though we'll miss her so much, and do sympathise with you too, we're all rejoicing with her in her joy at being with the Lord. My father Dr Stanley Smith, with be speaking at her funeral and I know hundreds of people will be there."* (Letter to Mr Hornby, February 9th, 1972)

Mrs Nora Lyth added in a note, *"I have a photo taken of her a few days before she died, sitting on the veranda, surrounded by Hornby High School girls in their green uniform who came to visit her when she was pretty ill and old. Also, when she was very frail, I was saying good night, when she said, 'Can you sleep on the mattress tonight, I can't bear to think of the shock of my servant girl finding me gone in the morning.' And of course I did, and she went to Heaven during the night."* A hint of the danger and tension at that time is at the end of the note, *"Incidentally the Secretary General said she must be buried in the Churchyard but he had to get out of the country urgently the next day for his safety."* (August 2002)

Arrangements were started for her funeral. Bishop Lyth's suggestion that she should be buried in the Town Cemetery was brushed aside by the Archdeacon who said, *"What take her from her home, no! no! no! She'll sleep with us, we all loved her and want her here."* (Nora Lyth, letter to Mr Hornby, February 9th 1972.) Instead, a grave was dug on a grassy slope in Cathedral ground, near the upper road. News was sent out far and wide, by telegram to the C.M.S. in London, over the Uganda radio and in the newspapers.

---

[8] Our researches have not traced which of her brothers this was, and Mrs Nora Lyth addressed him simply as "Mr Hornby". We hope that the publication of this book may lead to some contact with her family.

Miss Lilian Clarke left Kampala, where she was now based, to see to Miss Hornby's personal affairs. The author remembers being called to her house and asked to choose something by which to remember her. Miss Hornby had very few worldly possessions, just a few plates and cutlery, cooking pots, her bedding and books and her stick. There were pictures and the wooden plaque "RABBONI" which I chose, and later I gave it to Bishop Kivengere Girls' School, Muyebe, in memory of her. Miss Madge Quinn inherited her wooden towel-horse.

The *Uganda Argus* of February 10th carried an article "Angel of Mercy Dead" with a photograph taken in 1966 of Miss Hornby wearing a hat. The reporter wrote, *"In 1968, when I interviewed her at her home in Kigezi, Miss Hornby told me: 'If I die, my people will bury me.' And her dream has come true. Her thousands of friends, former students among them, will be at her burial. 'I like the Bakiga, the Bakiga are very kind to me, help me in everything and treat me like a queen' she once told me. Miss Hornby, although a Briton, was regarded by many as a Mukiga. 'She ate with us, drank with us and discussed her problems with us,' said a former student who was in tears . . . The funeral will take place at Kabale on Monday at noon."* In the same article, Miss Lilian Clarke paid the first tribute, *"This has been a blow to the entire population of Kigezi. I came to know her and developed much liking for her. She was a great woman. She had devoted most of her life to serving people in Kigezi – particularly women."*

A four hour Funeral on 14th February, 1972

As predicted, a vast crowd of mourners of all ages and races climbed the Hill to pay their respects to dear old Miss Hornby. The only member of her family to attend was her niece, Mrs Beakbane, and her husband from Kenya. It was impressive to see Bishop Barnabas Halem'Imana from the Roman Catholic Church and several Indian traders in turbans at the service. Retired Bishop Shalita came from Ankole. Mr John Bikangaga, the former Rutakirwa, who had been deprived of his position and title during the last years of the Obote regime, and was now only the Chairman of the National Housing Corporation, was there with his wife Grace. She was running a hardware shop in Kampala. Tributes included one by Mrs Merabu Kivengere, wearing a long black dress, on behalf of the Old Girls. Dr Algie Stanley Smith gave the address, from which some quotations have been made earlier in this book.

He based his remarks on the text found in the popular book of devotions, *Daily Light*, for the evening of the day she died, *"Blessed are the dead who die in the Lord – they rest from their labours; for their works follow them."* (Rev. 14.13) He said, *"The result of those labours lives on in the lives of the girls she taught, in the homes into which they married, and which have deeply influenced the whole of Kigezi and beyond, and which we believe will go on working in the lives of their children scattered throughout Uganda. So when Jesus came to call her, she was ready. Again as in Daily Light in the words of St Paul, 'I am now ready to be offered, and the day of my departure is at hand. I have fought a good fight, I have finished my course, I have kept the faith.' (II Tim. 4.6-8) And Paul goes on to talk of the prize giving for all who like Kaaka Hornby have been victorious in the fight. How I would love to be at that prize giving and to see her, no longer bowed and frail but strong and upright in her resurrection body; see her going up to receive her prize from the Lord Jesus, and hear the hand clapping and the shouts of joy from the women and girls of Kigezi, as she goes forward for her reward."* He went on to tell the story of her life and concluded by highlighting three aspects of her character which stood out in his memory.

*"The first was **her love for the under-privileged**. It always hurt her sense of fair play to see how the people living in the great centres seemed to get all the advantages, and how the people of the villages were neglected. For many years she made it her practice, at Easter and at Christmas, to go away from Kabale with all its missionaries and visitors, and out to the remote villages of Bufumbira or Kinkiizi, and there, surrounded by the humble and unspoilt village folk, rejoice with them in the coming of our Lord and Master as a babe in Bethlehem, His death on the Cross for our sins and His glorious Resurrection at Easter. This in fact was the motive that made her leave the crowded and established work at Mengo with all the comforts of advancing civilisation and offer to join us in Kigezi.*

*"The second was **her dauntless courage**. She showed this in her youth and on to her old age. She would never give in. Kigezi was a wild and primitive country. Mission authorities in Kampala laid it down that no lady was to go out on safari alone. But she insisted and we heartily approved, on going out with a bunch of her girls all over the country seeking out the women and girls in their distant homes. And now in the evening time of her life with increasing weakness it was a familiar sight to see her slowly, at her own pace, walking up the steep hill to the Church, almost fiercely refusing any help or sympathy. This courage made her a very challenging person and she could be quite intolerant, whether with black or white, of insincerity or hypocrisy.*

*"And lastly was **her love for people as persons**. Her girls of course held first place in her heart. She followed their progress in learning and character*

into married life, and then on to their children, ever a wise counsellor and faithful friend; and they responded to her love. To the end of her life they would come and visit her, and her astonishing memory kept her in intimate touch with the members of each family and a deep concern for their welfare. So she has been taken from us. All of us who have seen her failing powers, and her suffering so bravely and uncomplainingly borne, can only rejoice that she is with the Lord, whom she longed for inexpressibly – with Christ which is far better. And now our prayer is that the women and girls of Kigezi, who have seen this dear lady in their midst from her early youth to the grave, will cherish her memory, and be challenged to follow her example of selfless service to the under-privileged, her courage as a good soldier of Jesus Christ, and her self-giving love for all those she was called to serve in the name of the same Master to whom she gave everything she had."

At the end of the long and solemn Service, her coffin was carried down the grassy slope and laid to rest in the grave. The huge crowd was silent, before everyone returned to their daily occupations, deeply moved by what they had shared.

MULTI-RACIAL CROWD AT MISS HORNBY'S FUNERAL, FEBRUARY 14TH 1972
[PHOTO: E. TRAILL]

Lessons to be learned from her life

Bishop Festo Kivengere once said, *"We cannot thank God enough for what she did."*[9] There is much to be learnt from Miss Hornby's life and she left a great legacy in Kigezi, in Uganda as a whole and in the wider world. We are asking some well known men and women of the 21st century to comment on that legacy for the benefit of those who come after us. Their contributions will be printed at the end of this book.

Miss Hornby was born in 19th century England and lived most of her life in the 20th century in the heart of Africa. She embodied much that was best of the Victorian age, its high standards and ideals, loyalty to Queen or King and country, family values and hard work. The Victorians were a young society with a high birth rate, like Uganda. People showed great enterprise and courage in exploring and developing the world to support the growing population. Miss Hornby retained her youthfulness until the end of her life. Typical Victorians could be rigid and paternalistic, but Miss Hornby was adaptable, mellowing as she grew older, and she treated everyone the same. She made friends easily and had a retentive memory, especially regarding her "girls". She valued punctuality and good manners. She had a great sense of fun with an optimistic outlook. She was always ready to rise to a challenge or call for help.

Such a person had to have a strong inner foundation. Miss Hornby had a deep faith in God as her heavenly Father and she knew that "With God all things are possible" (Matthew 19.26). She knew Jesus Christ as her Lord and Saviour, speaking of Him frequently as "My Master". She was very aware of her own sins and shortcomings, constantly seeking forgiveness from Him. Her prayers were simple, child-like and practical and she humbly relied on the prayers of others in her work and the spreading of the Good News of Jesus Christ. It is extraordinary how God used her to become the "Kigezi Girls' No. 1 Teacher"[10] when she had no paper qualifications save a short training as a midwife during the First World War. Her life is a proof that God can use anyone who wholeheartedly commits his or her life to serve Him. She knew that she needed to maintain her daily walk of faith by prayer and Bible study with regular worship in Church and fellowship with other believers. She lived simply and sacrificially, challenging us in our materialistic societies. She kept going steadily and unconsciously bore the fruit of the Spirit for all to see.

---

[9]   See Coomes, p. 42.
[10] Heading of article in *Uganda Argus* newspaper, August 25th, 1969.

Miss Hornby loved her people and devoted herself to them by listening and learning their ways. Mrs Esther Sharp wrote of her in 1954, on her retirement, *"She knew the Bakiga and Bahororo and the Banyarwanda of Bufumbira as no one else has ever done, and somehow she managed to enter into their lives and love them as few white people are able to do."*[11] Her people became her family, her close friends, colleagues and also leaders in Church and society. She would have loved to see the day, not long after she passed away, December 3rd, 1972, when Rev. Festo Kivengere was consecrated as the first African Bishop of Kigezi, combining his world-wide evangelistic ministry with the leadership of the Diocese. At his side, Merab developed her own gifts of vision and leadership and we can ask now whether Miss Hornby's teaching and example had anything to do with the promotion of women's ministry in the Anglican Church? Bishop Festo was a pioneer in the ordination of women to full parish ministry, and Merabu herself was an example and role model to many women and girls.

Although she followed the pattern of identification with the people and forming relationships as the best preparation for sharing the Gospel, Miss Hornby did not lose her own strong personality. She was respected for her practical wisdom, common sense, organising ability and practical skills. In passing, it is interesting to note that most of the buildings which were erected under her direction have been demolished. Her legacy lies in people's lives, which may be why flowers are often placed on her simple white-tiled grave today. It is passed by many

MISS HORNBY'S GRAVE DECORATED WITH FLOWERS, 2010.
[PHOTO: E. TRAILL]

---

[11] Article in *Uganda Church Review* 1954-55.

students every day, also other people, and one wonders if they reflect on her life and example.

In her work as a missionary she bridged health and education, delivering more than 1,000 babies, caring for leprosy sufferers, taking a turn at running the mission Hospital when necessary, overseeing the mission station as well as setting up a successful girls' boarding school. As a teacher, she was a firm disciplinarian but always fair and just. She may not have used up-to-date teaching methods, but she imparted a love of learning and sense of adventure to her girls. She loved to walk over the hills of Kigezi, covering thousands of miles to oversee schools in the villages. She took a tent and a party of her staff and girls with her on these "treks". Later, she used her car for prodigious journeys around the District. She liked to be amongst her people for major events in the Christian year, Christmas and Easter, and she chose to live amongst them in her retirement.

Although Miss Hornby was unique, her example is not beyond the reach of any of us. It is appropriate to close the story by quoting John Bunyan's Pilgrim Song, which she sang many times in her life, as a call to a new generation of wholehearted disciples of Jesus Christ:

He who would valiant be
'gainst all disaster,
let him in constancy
follow the Master.
There's no discouragement
shall make him once relent,
his first avowed intent
   to be a pilgrim.

Who so beset him round
with dismal stories,
do but themselves confound
– his strength the more is.
No foes shall stay his might,
though he with giants fight:
he will make good his right
   to be a pilgrim.

Since, Lord, Thou dost defend
us with Thy Spirit,
we know we at the end
shall life inherit.
Then fancies flee away!
I'll fear not what men say,
I'll labour night and day
to be a pilgrim.

After John Bunyan (1628-88)

Chapter Nine
1884 – 1972
THE LEGACY OF CONSTANCE HORNBY

How can one assess the inheritance which Miss Hornby handed on to future generations? She did not leave worldly wealth or many fine buildings to her successors, but this faithful, devoted servant of the Lord left more valuable treasures particularly in the lives of her girls and their children. The inheritance received from her has multiplied over the years. Many older people in Kigezi and beyond still treasure her name, follow her teaching and tell stories about her. There were aspects of her life which deserve to be more widely known, hence the writing of this book. In this final chapter we record the opinions and thoughts of a number of people who knew her personally, and others who can see the wider picture and reflect on the importance of her pioneering work in girls' education.

Mrs Esther Sharp, the wife of Dr Leonard Sharp, pioneer medical missionary in Kigezi, wrote an appreciation of Miss Hornby on the occasion of her official retirement in 1954.[1] She wrote, *"She was intensely loyal both to her God and to her King or Queen, and also to the powers that be either in Church or State. Truth and kindness were always on her lips and in her heart, and she was the most stimulating person I have ever known out here. She walked literally thousands of miles over these tremendous Kigezi hills before the roads were made, and later was to be seen everywhere her little car would take her. Besides her other work she found time to deliver numerous babies for she is a most experienced midwife. 'This is my thousandth,' I heard her say one night after a delivery many years ago. Colour of skin made no difference to Constance, all were HER babies and I remember how thrilled she was when her first 'grandchildren' began to come along. Her love for her Lord was very great and she rejoiced to be called upon to suffer for His sake. Sometimes it was hardship, and sometimes abuse, even from some of her 'children'. She never seemed to be discouraged whatever happened but just went on cheerfully doing what she thought God wanted her to do. Was there a call for help at the Leper Island? Constance Hornby was the first to volunteer;*

---

[1] Extract from the *Uganda Church Review 1954-55,* Winter Quarter, pp. 9-13.

never sparing herself in the service of those terribly afflicted people. 'Feet washing' was a job at which she excelled. Her teaching was always vivid and true to the Word of God. She was never moved from her Sure Foundation by any wind of doctrine but went straight forward towards the goal of His high calling. To God be the glory and the praise for the remarkable personality and consecrated life of His servant. She has been an inspiration to all of us and we are thankful for every remembrance of her."

"Venturesome Love" is the title of the contribution from the **Bishop of Kigezi, Rt Rev. George Katwesigye:** *"Would you, at some point in your life, leave your comfortable lifestyle and venture into the 'unknown' for the sake of the underprivileged, the vulnerable and marginalised groups of people, moreover in a foreign country? This was so with Miss Constance Hornby, a missionary from England, thousands of miles away. She was a fierce fighter for girls' education and for that reason she came to Uganda in 1916 and lived most of her life in Kigezi until she died in 1972.*

"Throughout the history of Uganda, missionary women fought for women's rights through the promotion of girls' education and women's clubs. We give many thanks to Miss Constance Hornby for her enormous contribution to girls' education in Kigezi District. Her main purpose and concern was the girl child. When she arrived, it was a real struggle as she would climb hills and mountains and move down valleys in search of these girls. She would go from home to home, requesting their parents to release them since girls were not yet considered fit to go to school, as local culture destined them only to get married and bear children. Society thought educating girls was a waste of time and resources (i.e. money).

"In doing all this, I notice that Miss Hornby was answering God's call. Through hard times, Constance searched for girls, many unwilling and fearful, and brought them to school. The school was later named after her – Hornby High School, in recognition of the enormous service she had rendered to the region of Kigezi.

"What can be said about the girls who studied under Miss Hornby? Talking to them and looking at them, many have become prominent people. They have worked in high profile offices in different capacities and have become professionals in all spheres of life – unlimited. Whenever and wherever you meet such girls, you feel proud of them; they have self esteem and feel confident in whatever they decide to do.

"Hornby girls were taught different life skills, in addition to academic studies. Such skills have modelled them into significant personalities, humble

and submissive, who have made excellent wives and mothers! They have made a tremendous contribution to this nation by looking after their homes and families and especially encouraging their own girls to go to school, as they did. Without this background, many girls would still be uneducated.

"It is worth noting that following Miss Hornby's efforts in girls' education many other girls' schools have emerged and developed in the Greater Kigezi and Ankole regions and elsewhere in Uganda, namely Bishop Kivengere Girls' School, Muyebe, near Kabale, Seseme Girls' School in Kisoro, Bweranyange Girls' School in Bushenyi and Mary Hill High School in Mbarara, to mention but a few.

"We shall live to remember Miss Constance Hornby."[2]

Miss Joan Hall, retired Headmistress of Hornby High School, Bweranyange and Kyebambe Girls' Schools, former Home Secretary of the C.M.S. Ruanda Mission, College Lecturer and evangelist in England and Uganda, reflects in this way:

"Where is Miss Hornby? Oh! She is walking to Kisoro to bring her girls back to school . . . Yes, there are elephants on that road, and yes, it is a long way . . . but she will bring them back. Then, the skins they are wearing will come off and be hung up, and they will not see them again until the end of term. They will wear the bottle green uniform of the school for all of the term. The girls are attending 'Kabale Girls' Primary School', for as yet there were no secondary schools for girls in the Diocese of Kigezi, this was to come later. Miss Hornby could not have dreamed how those girls were going to develop and take on leadership both in their own homes and in other fields. There was something different about 'Miss Hornby's girls'. The personal care she gave them showed in the way they responded to her and to her training. Later this school was re-named 'Hornby High School'. What is obvious to me is that Miss Hornby's girls were, and are, amazing."[3]

Writing from Fort Portal, where he is the Chancellor of the Mountains of the Moon University, **Professor Edward Rugumayo** reflects as a

---

[2]   Paper, 22nd December 2010. In his accompanying letter, Bishop George wrote, *"Miss Constance Hornby means a lot to us and we cannot write enough words to express the legacy she has left. It is our hope and prayer that this book will be a challenge to the modern youth, both in the Diocese of Kigezi and abroad, to serve our Lord Jesus Christ. It is also our prayer that God will enable the publication of this book as soon as possible."*

[3]   Joan Hall, letter written in Kampala, 27th August, 2010.

former Minister of Education on the impact made by Miss Hornby:
"This is a fitting tribute to Miss Constance Hornby's Christian and pioneering spirit, based on strong faith in Christ and exhibiting undying love for fellow humans, especially her 'girls' and the people of Kigezi in general. Qualities that make this book so real are the lengthy quotations from her letters, friends' letters and missionary reports and other publications. My wife Foibe used to mention Miss Hornby as the person who identified and brought her mother, Dorotiya, to school and to the Lord Jesus. I didn't know Miss Hornby had done and achieved so much, and that her life's mission had transformed so many women to lead productive Christian lives. Sadly, what is lacking in many of our lives today are the qualities of Christian love of our fellow humans, a pioneering spirit, faith in God and dedication to one's calling. These are the qualities which stand out in Miss Hornby's rich life."

Complementing these remarks, **Mrs Foibe Rugumayo** shows how her whole family of well-educated people owes a great deal to her mother's teacher and mentor: *"My earliest memory of Miss Hornby was in my childhood. Our home was on the outskirts of Kabira Mission Station, about two miles from the school. We were playing and running round our house when she walked in. 'Musibiregye baana!' ('Good afternoon children') she greeted us. We all scampered and ran away. It was the first time I had seen a white lady and so I was scared. On a positive note, I believe Mother acquired the value of education from her. Although Father did not go to school, he learnt reading and writing at church during Catechism. A few days later, on 20th October 1934, he received the gift of salvation. I was the first in my family of 13 children to come to a living faith in the Lord Jesus before 10 years of age. Father did not have enough income to put us all through school beyond what Primary 6 and the Vernacular Teacher Training College could offer. But God makes a way where there is no way: not only was I able by God's grace to be one of the three girls selected to go to Kyebambe, a prestigious girls' secondary school in the Western Region, but three years later I was selected to go to Gayaza High School, one of the top schools for girls in Uganda. Under the Ben Kiwanuka scholarship scheme I had a successful interview to go to the U.S.A. and secured a degree in History. Back in Uganda I was able to relieve my parents and assist with school fees to put my siblings through. One brother, John Biteete, got a degree in History and my young sister, Joy Margaret Tukahirwa, got a PhD. at Makerere University. She was able to assist many of our nieces and nephews to go to school and to find jobs through her support and contacts. When our daughter was born in Lusaka, Zambia, in 1976, my* *husband asked me to give her a name according to Tooro custom: 'Mbabazi' ('Grace') I said. Mother had told me that Miss Hornby used to say if she had been blessed to have a child she would have called her Mbabazi. Together with what I had gone through during pregnancy, it was a befitting name. I believe that Mother's value of education which pushed us forward to where we are is basically due to Miss Hornby's influence."*[4]

Charity Kivengere is another example of being the daughter of one of Miss Hornby's girls in the early years. She writes:

"HOW DID MISS HORNBY SHAPE AND INSPIRE THE GIRLS SHE TAUGHT?

"My mother Merabu Nyinenzangi Kivengere was introduced to school by Miss Hornby. This was in 1931. She came from Rukungiri to join the girls' school that Miss Hornby had started in Kabale.

"My mother had many stories of her childhood/past and many of them were full of Miss Hornby and the work she did in establishing girls' education in Kigezi. We grew up hearing about Hornby from the time we were small. At school, although we were not taught by her, we sang about her and were often reminded of what she did. Indeed her story was well engraved in our hearts. Most of us went through Hornby High School for our primary education and we were very proud of it because this was the best primary school in Kigezi.

"My mother described Miss Hornby as a very hard working woman who above everything emphasized cleanliness. In school, Hornby taught the girls how to keep the dormitories clean, how to wash clothes properly, cut their nails and wash their feet to avoid jiggers. Hornby was also a tough disciplinarian who was respected but also feared.

"Clearly Hornby was a role model because much of what my mother described about her, we the children saw in our mother. Cleanliness, neatness, order in the home, etiquette were all important qualities that became foundational to our home. Others who interacted with my mother also saw these qualities in her and sometimes referred to her as a 'muzungu'.[5] *Mother also laboured to pass on these disciplines to the many ladies she taught both in school and later in Mothers Union. A number of women refer to the example she set for them. We the children have taken on many of these qualities and practise them in our homes.*

---

[4] Paper with photographs received from Professor Edward and Mrs Foibe Rugumayo, November, 2010.

[5] *Muzungu* means a traveller, hence an expatriate in Uganda.

"Miss Hornby had a passion for girls' education and this is something that truly impressed and inspired my mother. She always remembered and talked about the determination as well as the struggles Miss Hornby went through to get girls into school. Despite this commendable effort however, my mother saw many of her peers drop out of school one by one because of challenges of distance and family pressures (prejudices about girls' education). My mother came to appreciate even at this early age, the hindrances to girls' education and she often talked about it passionately.

"Miss Hornby somehow saw the potential in my mother and she, with a number of other girls, was sent for teacher training at Buloba. Hornby then requested my mother after this training to go and start a girls' school at Kinyasano in Rukungiri. It was a tough undertaking for my mother, but Miss Hornby believed in her and I believe this inspired self belief in my mother as well. She managed to start the school. There was something about Miss Hornby which inspired loyalty and in a way my mother was following the example that her headmistress had set for them. She could not let her down. I believe that the example Miss Hornby had set, the training, the exposure, the experience of starting a girls' school, all led to the beginnings of a passion in my mother for girls' education.

"Hornby's strong belief in what she was doing, passion for the girl child, her self-sacrificing approach, her lack of fear and boldness truly rubbed off and onto many of the girls she taught. The fact that a young white lady could courageously come to Kigezi and fight for the education of girls, touched and moved people like my mother to continue with this commendable effort. Many also felt privileged to have been chosen to be amongst the first girls to benefit from the tremendous single-handed effort of this white woman. For my mother the experiences were unforgettable and it led her to seeing herself as a torchbearer, to continue the good work already started by Hornby.

"My mother went on to do home schooling for her own children when the family was living in remote Tanzania for a number of years. She taught her children Hope and Joy to the level of P3. She advocated for girls' education throughout her life and was the visionary behind the establishment of Hornby High School Senior, and Bishop Kivengere Girls' School, Muyebe."[6]

We interviewed **Bishop William Rukirande**, now aged 79 and living happily in retirement on his farm a few miles away from Kabale. He spoke first of his earliest memories of Miss Hornby. One Christmas in

---

[6] Paper written in Kampala, December 2010.

the 1940's when he was aged 10-12 years, he went to a service at St Peter's Church in Kabale. Someone announced, *"All children go out. Miss Hornby wants you."* He went with others up to the small old church building on the site of the present new Cathedral and there Miss Hornby taught them songs in Rukiga. Later, he began his career as a teacher. He completed Primary Six at Muyebe and went to another school as an uncertified and unlicensed teacher, but Miss Hornby, the Schools Supervisor, picked him out, sent him back to repeat Primary Six and then arranged for him to go to Bishop Stuart College, Mbarara, for four years of teacher training. His first post was at Burema, then he was sent to Nyakatare in Kinkiizi in 1960. There, he made friends with Miss Hornby in her retirement. He used to visit her small house with its roses in the garden frequently. He remembered that she had a car and used to drive alone to Kabale through Mafuga Forest. He once asked her, *"Don't you fear?"* *"No,"* she replied, *"I'm not alone. I'm with God."* She had a very strong faith. She attended the local church and the Vicar, Rev. Ereneseti Rutagarukayo, looked after her. She had many visitors to her home.

We asked Bishop William what young people could learn from Miss Hornby. He mentioned faithfulness, trustworthiness, being full of faith and love for people. She did not despise anyone and always offered a cup of tea to any visitor who came. She would not compromise with sin and could be quite fierce, pointing with her finger and saying, *"Naayanga, buzima, naayanga! Tinaasiima,"* meaning, *"I refuse, truly, I refuse! I do not thank you (for that behaviour)."* She walked with a stick, which was a decorated one, and she was physically strong, never ill until the end. She would be very shocked by the corruption in Uganda today and the unreliability of many people.

In summary, he said that Miss Hornby led a quiet life and did not talk openly about her faith or experience of salvation, in contrast to some other missionaries who were more open. She preferred to get on with her work but she had a very deep faith underlying her life.[7]

Canon Samuel Mfitumukiza, Head of the Theology and Divinity Department at Bishop Barham University College, Kabale, gives an academic perspective on Miss Hornby's contribution: *"Miss Hornby travelled extensively throughout Kigezi and was known locally as Nyakaishiki*

---

[7]   Interview with Bishop William Rukirande, 31st December, 2010.

meaning that she had no husband. She greatly helped in the education of Kigezi women in elementary subjects. The first girls whom she taught became the target for marriage for the educated young men in the area at that time. She taught them how to be good women, how to care for their homes and children, cleanliness and entertaining visitors.

"After establishing herself in Kabale, she extended her teaching to women throughout the whole District through 'Women's Clubs' set up at different church centres. She taught women cleanliness, literacy, cookery and good manners, especially in the 1930s – 1940s. Rugarama (Kabale), Seseme (Bufumbira), Kinyasano (Rujumbura) and Nyakatare (Kinkiizi) served as her centres for training women in those areas. For example, as a result of her teaching, Bafumbira women started to gain status and respect in Banyarwanda society. Miss Hornby became a respected figure among Bafumbira and Kigezi people as a whole for her notable work among women. For her hard work in educating girls and women, and supervising schools, the British Protectorate Government honoured her with the title M.B.E."[8]

Here is a word from the current Head Teacher of Hornby High School (Secondary), **Mrs Karungi Mpairwe Night:** *"Thanks – I thank the Almighty God for this book that has been written about our great grandmother, Miss Constance Hornby. Thanks be to God who enabled her to serve Him selflessly. She left the comforts of her homeland and her people, travelled far and chose this part of the country to establish a school for girls. She left a legacy of great love.*

"About the school – it started in 1923 as a Primary School and later 'gave birth' to a secondary school in 1981. We are an Advanced level, girls' secondary boarding school. Students sit for national examinations at both 'O' and 'A' levels and are awarded Uganda Certificate of Education and Uganda Advanced Certificate of Education respectively. The foundation body is the Church of Uganda, Diocese of Kigezi. The school employs 40 teachers, 12 non-teaching staff and 24 group employees who work in the grounds and kitchen. The student population is 500.

"The Blind Section – At present there are six boys and eight girls. Blind students are taught with the other students but they are faced with a number of challenges and practical needs. Most of these students come from very needy families which cannot afford the fees, or the purchase of basic essentials like

---

[8] Extract from thesis entitled "The coming of Christianity to Bufumbira, 1912-1980" by Rev. Samuel Mfitumukiza, 1989.

soap. The majority of blind girls depend on 'good Samaritan' girls who help them. The situation of the blind students is actually critical.

"Other comments – The school is trying to emphasise vocational subjects such as Home Management, Fine Art and Computer Science, but some facilities and equipment are lacking. These courses would enable us to produce students who can be self-reliant. If successful, it would be like a dream come true for us and for our great grandmother who started the school.

"Our school motto is 'MUKUNDANE' or 'Love one another' and our school vision, 'In faith we mould the girl child all round'."[9]

Another educationalist, **Miss Kirsti Paterson**, Head Teacher of Avoch Primary School in the Highland Region of Scotland for 25 years and former Chairman of the Association of Christian Teachers (Scotland) read the draft of this book and had this to say:

"This is a very readable account of a remarkable Christian lady, an extraordinary pioneer in missionary work, with a vision to start a girls' school. Constance Hornby loved the people she worked and lived with in the Kigezi district. Her zeal for mission work is evident in her 'safari' adventures in the villages and her adaptability when working amongst lepers. She certainly did not work a 35 hour week!

"From the start of this story, one can detect the emerging Christian character of Miss Hornby and how this strong Christian commitment enabled her to deal with varying situations in her life. As the author engages the reader, you become aware of Miss Hornby's dependence on her Lord and Master, her compassion for lost souls, her practical abilities and a strong sense of humour. This is reinforced in the many accounts, from students and people who knew her, contained in the chapters of the book. The concluding chapters document her retirement and leaving this scene of time. The reader is challenged by the simple, yet active Christian lifestyle of a highly motivated Christian worker.

"The book also contextualises the country where Miss Hornby worked – its geography, historical and political features. Simultaneously, reference is made to the events happening in Britain (1920 – 1970). The author's detail is informative and stimulating . . . profitable reading."

Lastly, a chance encounter at Entebbe Airport in January 2010 with human rights activist **Baroness Caroline Cox** led to a fruitful correspondence about this book. She found the time in her busy life to read some chapters and to write the following about Miss Hornby's biography:

---

[9]   Paper written in Kabale, December 2010.

"This story of Miss Hornby's life and work is humbling, moving and inspirational. A pioneering missionary, her letters bring alive the challenges confronting the men and women who had the courage to travel to remote places and to live in very tough conditions in order to fulfill their calling to take the Christian faith to those who had never heard the Good News of the Gospel.

"The extracts from her letters make compelling reading: evocative and detailed, the reader can almost feel that they are present, sharing the experiences and meeting the people so vividly described. As the story progresses from the early pioneering days into more recent times, many insights are given into the political, economic and cultural changes experienced by Uganda during recent decades.

"But 'through all the changing scenes of life', the indomitable character of Miss Hornby shines through the inevitable problems and disappointments as well as the remarkable achievements and successes. Two of the many tributes recorded in the book testify to her achievements and her personality:

- She was an extraordinary pioneer belonging to the early days of Uganda. She had great vision in starting girls' education: 'Educate a girl, educate a family'.
- My memory is of a great personality with a sense of fun.

"Her legacy is lasting, especially her contribution to the development of education for girls – ahead of her time, but now, in our day, recognised as of essential importance for the attainment of modern-day priorities such as those enshrined in the universally acknowledged 'Millennium Development Goals'. And her personality, with her courage, commitment, toughness and humour, enabled her to achieve her objectives despite formidable challenges.

"The book, which captures both her personality and her remarkable contributions to the development of Christianity and to girls' education, is very engaging in its personal intimacy and graphic descriptions of life in Uganda during a fascinating period of the history of that great and beautiful nation."

Richmond and Twickenham today

Thinking back to the early chapters of this book, it is most interesting to visit the places where Constance Hornby spent her childhood. Richmond upon Thames itself is a lively, attractive town with many beautiful old buildings which would have been there in her day. Holy

HOLY TRINITY CHURCH, RICHMOND, TODAY
[PHOTO: THANKS TO HOLY TRINITY CHURCH]

Trinity Church where she was baptised and grew up is thriving, its doors open to different groups on weekdays and it holds well-attended services on Sundays. It is particularly exciting, one could say

Providential, that on the very land where Mr Hornby's cows used to graze there is a modern Primary School with a Christian foundation. The prospectus of Holy Trinity Primary School describes it as *"A voluntary aided Church of England school for nursery, infant and junior children. It draws from the local community and has close links with Holy Trinity Church in Sheen Park, from which it takes its name. Its strong Christian foundation is expressed through worship, teaching and community."*[10] We can imagine how Miss Hornby would have loved to visit that school at her birthplace, and to talk to the children and teachers today. There is a spiritual and educational continuity here.

Across the River Thames in Twickenham, the house where the family lived at 7 Amyand Park Gardens is still there. It was unscathed in the bombings during the Second World War. St Stephen's Church where she was active as a young woman is flourishing today. It was the church from which she entered the service of the Church Missionary Society, but only a mention of her being sent out to Uganda could be found in the church archives, although a search through the parish magazines was made by the Missionary Secretary.

Searches for clues and links could go on and on. We are sad not to have had any contact with members of her family during our researches, but perhaps the publication and distribution of this book will yield some happy results in that part of the quest.

To sum up, Constance Hornby was like a runner in a relay race. She received the torch of Christian faith and education from others, ran with it bravely throughout her long life and passed it on to others. We conclude in timeless words which she would have known, *"Blessed are the dead which die in the Lord from henceforth: Yea, saith the Spirit, that they may rest from their labours; and their works do follow them."*[11]

---

[10] Holy Trinity Primary School, Carrington Road, Richmond, TW10 5AA, Prospectus (May 2005).

[11] Revelation 14 v. 13, quoted from the Authorised or King James Version of the Bible, 1611.

Appendix One
CHURCH MISSIONARY SOCIETY
GENERAL COMMITTEE MINUTE: 16TH November 1954

On a letter dated 4th August 1954 from Miss Constance Hornby to the Africa Secretary, the Africa Committee recommended the following resolution, which was adopted:

> That the retirement of Miss Constance Hornby, M.B.E., as from 31st October, 1954 be recorded.

Miss Constance Hornby was accepted by the Society as a missionary in full connection in July 1915 and in October of the following year she left England to join the Uganda Mission. In 1933, when the Ruanda Mission became distinct from the Uganda Mission, she came under Ruanda but continued to work on Uganda territory. Miss Hornby who came home this year for the first time in eighteen years retires from 31st October 1954.

Miss Hornby began her overseas service in education at Iganga Girls' Boarding School. From there she moved, after a short time, to Gayaza, then to Kampala and in 1925 to Kabale where the greater part of her missionary life has been spent. Before she left for furlough she was helping with the supervision of the Girls' Boarding School there and that furlough was delayed for a month so that she might be presented to Her Majesty the Queen before coming home. Miss Hornby had the distinction of being the first missionary to retire on completion of full service.

Throughout her long and devoted service this missionary gave herself wholeheartedly and unstintingly to the education of the African boys and girls who came under her care, bringing to them not only the learning of the school-book, but also the Gospel message of a loving Saviour. In 1948 public reception was given of Miss Hornby's contribution to African education in the award in the New Year's Honours List of the M.B.E.

In bidding farewell to Miss Hornby the Committee gave thanks to God for her life of unselfish and loyal service overseas and assure her of continued prayerful remembrance in the Society's wide fellowship as she returns to East Africa to continue that service.

Appendix Two
SOME HYMNS AND SONGS

These meant a lot to Miss Hornby and are mentioned in the book.

1   Hymn 230 in the Runyankore-Rukiga Prayer Book, a local modification of an old hymn which was probably sung in the churches Miss Hornby attended when she was young.

We are soldiers of Christ, who is mighty to save

1   TURI abaserukare ba Kristo Yesu,
Niwe Manzi y'okutujuna;
Niw' atwebember' omu rugamba rwona,
Kandi turwan' ahabw'amaani ge.

2   Tukaragaana nawe kub' abeesigwa,
Kuguma nitumworobera.
Ka tugyende nawe, tuteer' abazigu,
Tubone kukiza beene waitu.

3   Ku turaajwar' eby'okurwanisa byaitu,
Rurara n'engabo n'enkaito,
Tituritiina muzigu ween' omubi;
Turyasinguz' amaani ga Yesu.

4   Titurikwenda kuba bairu b'ekibi,
Abategyekw' eby'omubiri;
Turi abaana ba Yes' abu yaacungwire,
Kandi titukitegyekw' Omubi.

5   Ka tugume tuhweran' omu rugamba,
Habw'okuba turi ihe rimwej
Turi ishe-emwe, abain' amatsiko gamwe,
Nituramy' Omukam' omwe wenka.

6   Habw'amaani ga Yesu turyasingura,
Turwan' okuhitsy' aha mperu;
Bwanyima turyaheebw' ebihembo bindi.
Kandi Ruhang' aryatuhuumuza.

Original words by Thomas B. Pollock, English version in the Supplement to Hymns Ancient and Modern, 1889:

We are soldiers of Christ, who is mighty to save,
And His banner the Cross is unfurled;
We are pledged to be faithful and steadfast and brave
Against Satan, the flesh, and the world.

We are brothers and comrades, we stand side by side,
And our faith and our hope are the same;
And we think of the Cross on which Jesus has died,
When we bear the reproach of His Name.

At the font we were marked with the Cross on our brow,
Of our grace and our calling the sign;
And the weakest is strong to be true to his vow,
For the armour we wear is divine.

We will watch ready armed if the Tempter draw near,
If he comes with a frown or a smile;
We will heed not his threats, nor his flatteries hear,
Nor be taken by storm or by wile.

We will master the flesh, and its longings restrain,
We will not be the bond slaves of sin,
The pure Spirit of God in our nature shall reign,
And our spirits their freedom shall win.

For the world's love we live not, its hate we defy,
And we will not be led by the throng;
We'll be true to ourselves, to our Father on high,
And the bright world to which we belong.

Now let each cheer his comrade, let hearts beat as one,
While we follow where Christ leads the way;
'Twere dishonour to yield, or the battle to shun,
We will fight, and will watch, and will pray.

Though the warfare be weary, the trial be sore,
In the might of our God we will stand;
Oh! what joy to be crowned and be pure evermore,
In the peace of our own Fatherland.

2 *"Tukutendereza Yesu"*

The theme-song of the East African Revival which originated amongst Luganda-speaking Christians. It was based on an English hymn popular at the Keswick Convention and thus well-known by the early missionaries in Kigezi. This Luganda version, and English translation, are supplied by Rev. Dr Manuel Muranga.

"Omusayi ogw'omuwendo omungi"

1 YESU Mulokozi wange
   Leero nze wuwo wekka;
   Omusaayi gwo gunnaazizza,
   Yesu Mwana gw'endiga.
   Tukutendereza, (n'ebirala).

   Tukutendereza, Yesu
   Yesu Mwana gw'endiga;
   Omusaayi gwo gunnaazizza
   Nkwebaza, Mulokozi.

Jesus my Saviour,
I am now yours alone,
Your blood has washed me,
Jesus, the Lamb.

We praise you, Jesus:
Jesus, The Lamb;
Your blood has washed me;
I thank you, Saviour.

2 Edda nafuba bufubi
   Okufuna emirembe;
   Leero mmaliridde ddala
   Okweyabiza Yesu.
   Tukutendereza, (n'ebirala).

In the past I merely tried
To find peace;
But now I am determined
To give myself wholly to Jesus.

3 Nnaababuuliranga abantu
   Obulokozi bwonna
   Obutali bwa kitundu
   Obulamba obw'obuwa.
   Tukutendereza, (n'ebirala).

I shall tell people
About salvation in its fullness;
Not about a partial salvation,
But about one that is complete
   and free.

4 Nnaategeezanga ebya Yesu
   N'obuvumu ne sitya;
   Eyanzigya mu busibe
   N'okuwonya eyamponya.
   Tukutendereza, (n'ebirala).

I shall tell of Jesus
With courage, fearing nothing;
Of Him who took me out of
   captivity
And even healed me.

5 Neebaza eyannunula nze
   Eyamponya wa kisa!
   Yesu ankuuma ansanyusa era,
   Bulijjo yeebazibwe.
   Tukutendereza, (n'ebirala).

I thank Him Who redeemed me;
He Who healed me is gracious!
Jesus keeps me and gives me joy,
Thanks be to Him always!

The original in English was No. 170 in the Keswick Hymn Book, "Cleansing Blood" – by L.M. Rouse, music by D. Boole:

> Precious Saviour, Thou hast saved me;
> Thine, and only Thine, I am;
> Oh, the cleansing blood has reached me!
> Glory, glory to the Lamb!
> Glory, glory hallelujah!
> Glory, glory to the Lamb!
> Oh, the cleansing blood has reached me!
> Glory, glory to the Lamb!

3 The Heart: Hornby High School Secondary Anthem

As Hornby High School developed, an anthem about the founder was written and is sung by the school today.

> Hornby the courageous woman
> Wonderful what she did
> She will ever be remembered
> For all times now and evermore.
>
> Let us sing and praise her name
> For the duty she did
> Her name shall always be remembered
> The name Hornby sounds so great.
>
> *It was started as a primary school*
> *In 1923, and developed*
> *Into a secondary school in 1981.*
>
> We are students of Hornby High School
> We swear we maintain
> The rules and real education
> Our great grandmother did show.

BIBLIOGRAPHY

Introduction
Aldrich, Joe: *Lifestyle Evangelism*, Multnomah Books, Sisters, Oregon 1993.
Morisy, Ann: *Journeying Out,* Morehouse Publishing, London 2004.

Chapter One 1884-1901
Anon. author: *Holy Trinity Church, Richmond, Surrey 1870-1970*, Holy Trinity Church, Sheen Park, Richmond TW9 1UP, 1970.
Baptisms in Holy Trinity, Richmond, 14 August 1880 - 9 March 1893, Surrey History Centre, Woking.
Book of Common Prayer (c. 1901-1910), Oxford University Press.
England and Wales Delineated (c. 1840): Vol. IV p. 1334 "Richmond, a Village", pub. at the Steam Press of W.H. Cox, Lincoln's Inn Fields, London.
Fraser, Maxwell: *Surrey*, Batsford, London 1975.
Freeman M. and Aldroft D.: *The Atlas of British Railway History*, Croom Helm, London 1985.
Godfrey, Alan: *Richmond Hill and East Sheen 1894, Old Ordnance Survey Maps with Notes*, A. Godfrey Maps, Consett.
Greater London Atlas, Fifth Edition (c. 1935), Geographia, London.
Hughes, M.V.: *A London Family 1870-1900*, Oxford University Press 1946.
Landranger Map: West London, revised 2002, Ordnance Survey, Southampton.
Leepman, Michael (ed.): *Eyewitness Travel Guide: London*, Dorling Kindersley, London 1993, 2003 edn.
Mandela, Nelson: *Long Walk to Freedom*, Abacus, London 1994.
Mingay, G.E.: *The Transformation of Britain 1830-1939*, Paladin Grafton, London 1987.
Reader, W.J.: *Victorian England*, Batsford, London 1964.
Smellie, Alexander: *Evan Henry Hopkins: A Memoir*, Marshall Bros. London 1920.

Chapter Two 1901-1916
Cable, M. and French, F.: *Ambassadors for Christ*, Hodder and Stoughton, London 1937.
Ensor R.C.K.: *England 1870-1914*, Oxford University Press 1936.
Gollock, G.A.: "Training of Women Missionaries", in the *Church Missionary Intelligencer,* C.M.S. 1898.
Pollock, J.C. with Randall, I.: *The Keswick Story*, Christian Literature Crusade, Fort Washington 2006
Stock, E.: *One Hundred Years: Being the Short History of the C.M.S.*, Church Missionary Society, 6 Salisbury Square, London 1898.

Chapter Three 1916-1922

Cook, Sir Albert: *Uganda Memories 1897-1940*, Uganda Society, Kampala 1945.

Girls' Friendly Society Archives: "Overseas Empire Education Committee 1927-36" and *G.F.S. Magazine 1921*, at the Women's Library, London.

Guillebaud, Lindesay: *A Grain of Mustard Seed: the Growth of the Ruanda Mission of C.M.S.*, Ruanda Mission, 7 Wine Office Court, Fleet Street, London, EC4, 1959.

Makower, Katharine: *Not a Gap Year but a Lifetime* Apologia Publications, Box 3005, Eastbourne, BN21 9BS, 2008.

Miller, Charles: *The Lunatic Express*, Macdonald, London 1971.

Oldham, J.H.: *Florence Allshorn and the Story of St Julian's*, Hodder & Stoughton, London 1951.

Pirouet, M. Louise: *Black Evangelists: Spread of Christianity in Uganda 1891-1914*, Rex Collins, London 1978.

St John, Patricia: *Breath of Life: the Story of the Ruanda Mission*, The Norfolk Press, 19 Draycott Place, London 1971.

Stanley, Henry M.: *Through the Dark Continent*, Vol. 1, Greenwood, New York 1978, 1969 edn.

Stuart, Mary: *Land of Promise: The Story of the Church in Uganda*, Highway Press, 6 Salisbury Square, London 1957.

Thomas and Scott: *Uganda*, Oxford University Press 1939.

Thomas, H.B.: *The Story of Uganda*, Oxford University Press 1939.

Chapter Four 1923-1930

Aldrich, Joe: *op. cit.*

Carswell, Grace: *Cultivating Success in Uganda: Kigezi Farmers and Colonial Policies*, British Institute for Eastern Africa, London 2007.

Church, J.E.: *Quest for the Highest*, Paternoster Press, Exeter 1981.

Denoon, Donald (ed.): *A History of Kigezi in South-West Uganda*, National Trust Adult Education Centre, Kampala, Uganda c. 1972.

Girls' Friendly Society: *G.F.S. Magazine 1922-1930*, in the Women's Library, London.

Mbiti, John S.: *African Religions and Philosophy*, Heinemann, London 1969

Ngologoza, Paulo: *Kigezi and its Peoples*, East Africa Literature Bureau, Nairobi 1969.

Ruanda Notes: Magazine of the Ruanda Mission C.M.S., from 1922 onwards, in the Archives Department of the Church Mission Society, Watlington Road, Oxford.

Chapter Five 1930-35

Annual Reports 1925-61, Uganda Government Dept of Education, in Cambridge University Library.

Church, J.E.: *op. cit.*

Education in East Africa: Report of the Second African Education Commission, Phelps Stokes Fund 1925, in Cambridge University Library.

Girls' Friendly Society: *G.F.S. Magazine 1931-35*, in the Women's Library, London.
Golden Bells, Children's Special Service Mission (Scripture Union), London 1925.
Houghton, Frank: *Amy Carmichael of Dohnavur*, S.P.C.K., London 1953.
Ruanda Notes: Magazine of the Ruanda Mission C.M.S. from 1930-33, in the Archives
    Dept of the Church Mission Society, Oxford.

Chapter Six 1936-46

Carswell, Grace: *op. cit.*
Church, J.E.: *op. cit.*
Coomes, Anne: *Festo Kivengere*, Monarch Publications, Eastbourne 1990.
Girls' Friendly Society: *G.F.S. Magazine 1936-46*, in the Women's Library, London.
Hicks, Laurel (ed.) *The Modern Age: the History of the World in Christian Perspective*
    Vol. II, Chapter 18 "The World Wars", Beka Book Publications, USA 1981.
Ruanda Notes: Magazine of the Ruanda Mission C.M.S. 1936-46, in the Archives
    Dept. of the Church Mission Society, Oxford.

Chapter Seven 1946-66

CMS Newsletter 1939-46, written by the General Secretary, Church Missionary
    Society, London.
Coomes, Anne: *Festo Kivengere*, Monarch Publications, Eastbourne 1990.
Golden Bells, *ibid.*
Ingrams, Harold: *Uganda*, Corona Library, HMSO, London 1960.
Mushaija, Jolly: *History of Hornby High School*, booklet printed at the school in
    Kabale, 1997.
Ruanda Notes: Magazine of the Ruanda Mission C.M.S. 1946-66 in the Archives
    Dept of the Church Mission Society, Oxford.
The Royal Visit to Uganda 1954, Uganda Government, Kampala 2007.

Chapter Eight 1966-72

Aldrich, Joe: *op. cit.*
Daily Light (1959), Samuel Bagster & Sons, London.
Makower, K.: *op. cit.*
Morisy, Ann: *op. cit.*
Museveni, Y.K.: *Sowing the Mustard Seed*, Macmillan, London 1997.

INDEX